ABOUT THE AUTHOR

Patrick C. Dorin came by his interest in railroads at an early age. While still at Northland College in Ashland, Wisconsin, he worked for the Great Northern, then the Elgin, Joliet & Eastern RR, and finally the Milwaukee Road. Dorin has degrees in elementary education and school administration and curriculum, and is working for his Doctors degree.

However, the rail bug still has a tight hold on him, and he continues to prepare an average of one major rail pictorial history a year. "Milwaukee Road East" is his tenth title published by Superior. His earlier books include "The Grand Trunk Western Railroad," "Everywhere West: The Burlington Route," "Canadian Pacific Railway," "Chicago and Northwestern Power," "The Canadian National Railways' Story," "Coach Trains and Travel," "Domeliners," "Commuter Railroads" and a handbook for young rail fans, "The Young Railroader's Book of Steam."

The Milwaukee Road East

The typical passenger train of a century ago looked like this
Chicago, Milwaukee & St. Paul consist photographed at
Oconomowoc, Wisconsin about 1878. (The Milwaukee Road)

The Milwaukee Road East

America's Resourceful Railroad

By
Patrick C. Dorin

Superior PUBLISHING COMPANY

Library of Congress Cataloging in Publication Data

Dorin, Patrick C.
  Milwaukee Road East.

  Includes index.
  1. Chicago, Milwaukee, St. Paul, and Pacific
Railroad.   I. Title.
HE2791.C671347   385′.0978   78-3834
ISBN 0-87564-528-3

FIRST EDITION

PRINTED IN THE UNITED STATES OF AMERICA

Dedicated To
My Aunt and Uncle
Sydney and Sophie Maebius

FOREWORD

Milwaukee Road East takes a brief look at the company's early development and construction, but concentrates on a pictorial review of the trains, traffic and passenger travel on the lines east of Harlowton, Montana. Individual chapters cover the passenger, mail and gas-electric trains from the standard era through the domeliners and finally to Amtrak. Other chapters look at the great "Hiawatha" and commuter fleets of Chicago and Milwaukee. Freight service throughout the midwest from Southern Indiana to Nebraska and Montana include time freights, piggyback and flexi-van services, the heavy coal and ore trains, logging and last but not least, the patrol — the Milwaukee Road's version of the way freight.

The book concentrates on the period of time from the 1920's through the mid-1970's and includes much of the equipment required to carry the thousands of passengers and tons of freight traffic over Milwaukee trackage. This is the story of a fine rail system many of whose innovations were later implemented by other lines. Still others, such as the totally unique observation cars that drew thousands of passengers, were never emulated by other companies. It all added up to an unusual personality, and provided the substance for the company's motto, "America's Resourceful Railroad."

Patrick C. Dorin

North Branch, Minn.
Feb. 24, 1977

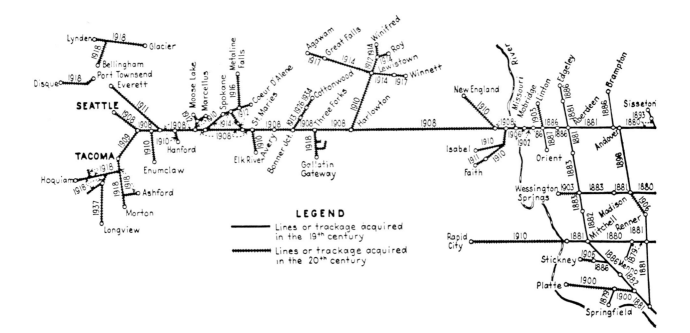

TABLE OF CONTENTS

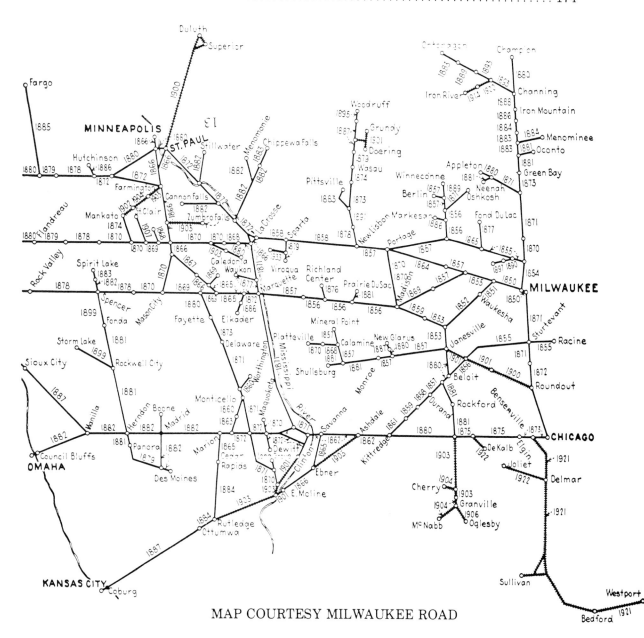

MAP COURTESY MILWAUKEE ROAD

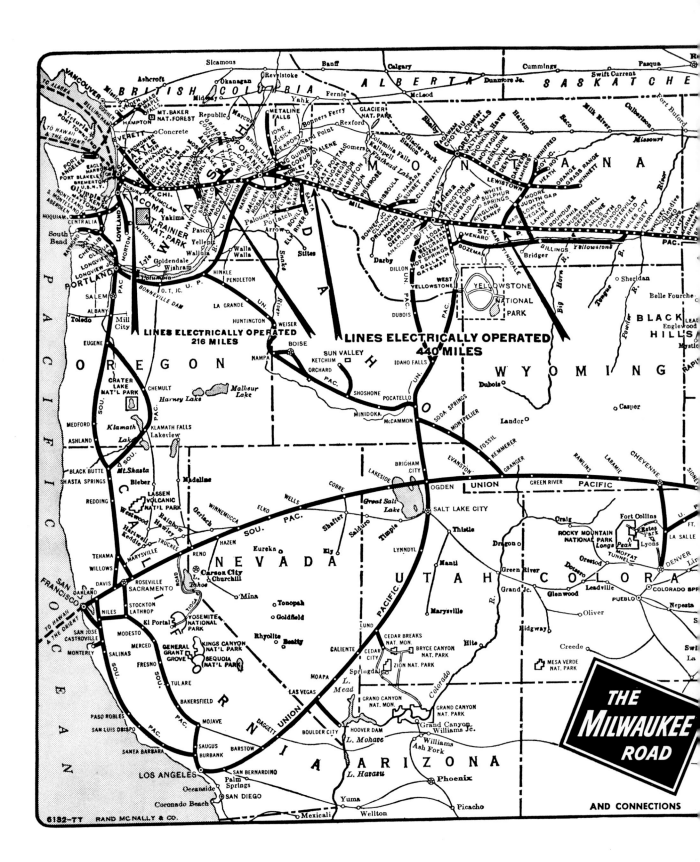

THE MILWAUKEE ROAD

AND CONNECTIONS

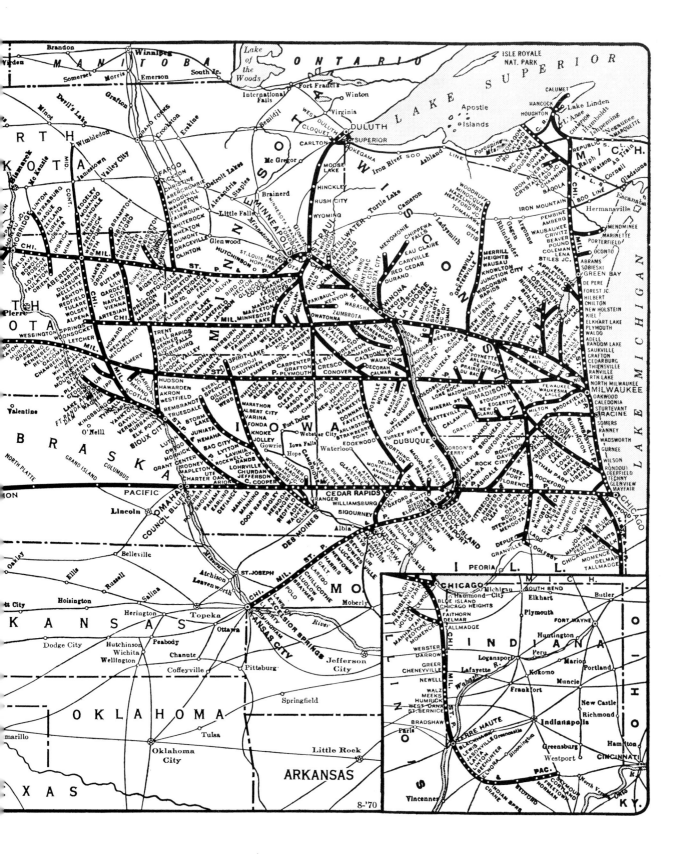

ACKNOWLEDGMENTS

This writer would like to thank the following people for their kind assistance with *Milwaukee Road East.*

Albert P. Salisbury of Superior Publishing Company for his encouragement and work with the layout through to the final publication of the book.

My wife Karen who always spends a great deal of her time checking and rechecking materials, photos and the manuscript.

Luther Miller of Railway Age for permission to use Railway Age and Railway Age Gazette from 1890 to 1976 as resource materials.

Sy Dykhouse for his superb map work.

The staff of the Milwaukee Road who provided this writer not only with encouragement, but also numerous photos and various types of materials and data for the undertaking.

Photographs came from many sources including the following: Paul Stringham, Harold K. Vollrath, Russ Porter, Al Paterson, Dick George, William S. Kuba, Jim Scribbins, Delta County Historical Society, William A. Raia, A. Robert Johnson and John H. Kuehl.

Pullman-Standard and Thrall Car Manufacturing Company also assisted the writer with photographs.

The dust jacket painting was done by Russ Porter.

Thanks must also go to the staff of the Minnesota Photo Company in Cambridge for their fine work in photo printing.

Without the tireless assistance of these fine people, the book simply could not have been written.

The author apologizes if any acknowledgment has been left out inadvertently.

Chapter 1
Historical and Geographical Development of Lines East

One of the USA's most remarkable transcontinental railroads — *The Milwaukee Road* — began as a small local line with only a goal of being a trans-Wisconsin route. Psychologically, this was the reverse of so many roads, which originally thought of building a vast system, and yet ended up as obscure short lines to die off before their first decade. The Milwaukee, on the other hand, grew from a trans-Wisconsin route to a Midwest-Pacific Northwest transcontinental railroad accomplishing it in such a way as to give credence to its reputation as *America's Resourceful Railroad*.

During the 1840's, settlers were moving into the area west of Milwaukee all the way to the Mississippi River. The result was a building up a freight traffic that was handled by wagon over poorly constructed roads. Eventually the farm produce traffic became so heavy that the teamsters could not handle it, and much of the food rotted before reaching a market. Clearly, there was only one solution — a railroad, although an attempt would be made to build a canal first. Byron Kilbourn, the son-in-law of John Fitch (one of the inventors of the steamboat), succeeded in getting the United States to grant land to the canal company, and a few attempts were made to begin construction. However, the canal failed before it even got started.

Kilbourn was a far-sighted man, and decided to turn his failure into a success by obtaining a charter for the Milwaukee and Waukesha Railroad in 1847. The authorized capital was $100,000, and the charter permitted the road to be constructed from Milwaukee to Madison, and then later to some point on the Mississippi River.

Grading was begun in the fall of 1849, and was carried on for nearly a whole year, almost without cash, but with the barter system. Farmers paid in cattle, horses, beef, pork, wheat and other goods; many people paid in labor, for which in turn they all received stock. Finally a group of about 100 farmers mortgaged their farms for the cash that was needed to complete the railroad and place it in operation.

Grading was completed by the middle of 1850, and five miles of track were laid by November. On November 20th, the directors and prominent Milwaukee citizens were taken for a ride on the first railroad in Wisconsin, in two open freight cars behind "Number 1." The Milwaukee Road has designated this date as the anniversary of the beginning of its service.

February 25, 1851 marked the first formal trip to Waukesha, 20 miles from Milwaukee, with the usual fanfare of band music, addresses, fireworks and dinners. By April 2, 1851, twice-daily train service in each direction was being provided by the new company.

The name was changed to the Milwaukee and Mississippi Railroad on February 1, 1850 and it was decided that Prairie du Chien should be the goal, primarily because it was the point from which the Pacific railroad projected by Asa Whitney would take off.

The M & M was open to Prairie du Chien on April 15, 1857. The first train through consisted of new passenger equipment (built by the company shops in Milwaukee) and was welcomed to the shores of the Mississippi River by a 200 gun salute. To symbolize the new railroad, an eight-gallon keg of Lake Michigan water was emptied into the Mississippi. Two years later, the railroad installed ferry service at Prairie du Chien, with "The Lady Franklin," a craft that was built to sail on water or run on ice.

A financial panic swept the U.S.A. in 1857, and the result was the receivership of the M & M on May 9, 1859. In early 1861, the property was purchased by the Milwaukee & Prairie du Chien for $7.5 million. The panic also brought foreclosure on the farm mortgages that provided some of the original financing. Much bitterness prevailed over this, and finally led to grangerism and restrictive legislation by not only Wisconsin but other states and the Federal Government as well. These restrictions still plague the railroad industry today.

The next man to figure in the new company's history was Alexander Mitchell, a Milwaukee banker. He took over the Chicago & Milwaukee (a predecessor of the Chicago & North Western) the Milwaukee & Prairie du Chien and the La Crosse

An unusual part of the Milwaukee Road history was the narrow gauge operations in the Cascade, Iowa area. The photos were taken in the 1925-26 era, and four of the locomotives carried the series 1 thru 4, a set of numbers that would become world famous in the streamlined Atlantics a decade later.

& Milwaukee, which had been reorganized as the Milwaukee and St. Paul. In 1866, Mitchell became president of the Milwaukee & Prairie du Chien, which in turn set the wheels in motion for the sale of the M&PdC to the M&StP on December 31, 1967. The new company kept the name of the Milwaukee and St. Paul and operated 820 route miles and was the largest railroad in the mid-west at the time. It operated 125 locomotives, 122 passenger cars and 2,248 freight cars. By 1867, the company had extended to the Twin Cities via Calmar and to Chicago by 1872. In February, 1874, the name of the company was changed to Chicago, Milwaukee & St. Paul (a title it was to keep until 1928).

In 1880 the company leased the Chicago & Pacific, giving it a route from Chicago to Savanna, Illinois and Sabula, Iowa. The company had now grown to 3,775 miles with 425 locomotives, 319 passenger cars and 13,315 freight cars.

Alexander Mitchell died in 1887, and the leadership of the Milwaukee went to Roswell Miller. He took over the system of 5,670 miles spreading over five states and the Dakota Terribory. The headquarters had shifted from Milwaukee to Chicago in 1889 and 1890. The company had seven bridges crossing the Mississippi and Missouri Rivers, as well as a large number of grain elevators and warehouses.

The Milwaukee had a very independent nature, and fought continuously against being pulled in by eastern financial men. The company had operated its own sleeping cars, and manufactured its own rolling stock and locomotives. However, the 1870's saw the road pulled by Philip D. Armour and William D. Rockefeller. Henry Flagler also got into the act. The aim of the struggle was to keep Hill and Morgan out of Chicago, a goal in which they were joined by E. H. Harriman of the Union Pacific. Since the Milwaukee Road linked both Omaha and the Twin Cities with Chicago, the struggle to retain independence was difficult. The problem did not cease until Morgan and Hill secured control of the Burlington, which allowed the Northern Pacific and Great Northern entrance to Chicago. Oh, how different history might have been if the GN and/or NP had not succeeded in getting the Burlington!

In 1899 Albert J. Earling took over the presidency from Miller. He had been a Milwaukee railroad man since the age of 17, and was a pioneer in the development of the block signal system. He was noted for his knowledge of men.

Earling took over a 6,154 mile railroad reaching as far west as Bowdle, South Dakota and only 40 miles short of the Missouri River. The independent nature of the road urged it to build to the Pacific Coast and authorization was received by the board on November 28, 1905. A whole new era began,

The narrow gauge line was 36 miles long, built in 1879-80 and acquired by the Milwaukee in late 1880. Operating between Cascade and Bellevue, the line lost considerable amounts of money and was subsequently sold in 1933, only to be totally abandoned in 1936. The three-foot gauge line owned 4 locomotives and over 100 freight cars. (Harold K. Vollrath Collection)

which was covered in *The Milwaukee Road West* by Charles and Dorothy Wood, published by Superior Publishing Company in 1972.

However, new territory was not left untapped on the lines east. The Milwaukee Road leased the Chicago, Terre Haute & Southeastern Railroad in 1921 and the Chicago, Milwaukee and Gary in 1922 under the guidance of President Harry E. Byram. Byram had taken over from President Earling in 1917, and interestingly enough, he came from the Burlington Route. The CTH&SE became an integral part of the Milwaukee Road in 1948.

But clear sailing was not to be for the Milwaukee Road. On March 18, 1925, the company went into receivership. Byram, Mark W. Potter and Edward J. Brundage were appointed the receivers. The following day Milwaukee common stock was sold at a low of $5.00 compared to 199 and ⅝ twenty years previously.

There were two principal reasons for the bankruptcy. The Northwest was experiencing adverse economic conditions and the company had a top-heavy financial structure. There were other factors too, such as the opening of the Panama Canal in 1914, which destroyed much of the road's transcontinental traffic before it could begin to exploit its costly Pacific Coast extension.

On March 31, 1927, the Chicago, Milwaukee, St. Paul and Pacific Railroad was organized to acquire the property. On January 13, 1928, H. A. Scandrett took over as president.

But the Milwaukee was to receive one more blow — the great depression. Agriculture was hit hard; the drought and dust storms compounded the picture as did the government restrictions mentioned earlier. The ICC handed down a decision in May, 1930 which had the effect of driving high-rated short haul traffic to the trucks and decreasing revenues on the staple traffic of the railroads. It would almost seem that the ICC and the State and Federal Governments were out to give the subsidized forms of transport (air and highway) the cream of the railway traffic.

The result of all of this was one more bankruptcy. In June of 1935, a petition was filed and in October, H. A. Scandrett, Walter J. Cummings and George L. Haight were appointed trustees. The trusteeship was to last for a decade through complicated planning, lawsuits, the last half of the depression, World War II, the development of the Hiawatha and many other things that put together a rather complicated drama of conflicting events. It is highly interesting, though, that through all of this, the company placed in service a

A Milwaukee Road oddity was the pontoon bridge over the Mississippi River at Marquette, Iowa. Now dismantled, this photo shows the bridge in open position. The state of Iowa is on the right. (Paul Stringham)

fleet of Hiawatha streamliners (built by the company shops) that have gone down in history as among the nation's finest. What is so impressive is that no matter how bad things got, the Milwaukee Road always put its best foot forward.

Shortly after the war, the company was finally reorganized and Scandrett resumed its presidency. Leo T. Crowley became chairman of the board.

After leading the company through some of its most trying years, Scandrett retired in 1947, with C. H. Buford, a Milwaukee Road man since 1907, succeeding. His tenure was short as he was succeeded September 1, 1950 by John P. Kiley, who had first joined the road in 1913. Kiley vigorously continued the program of dieselization, speeding up freight service, improving the Hiawathas and other passenger trains, and eliminating the unprofitable branches as well as other financial burdens. Kiley also had the pleasant task of taking over at the time of the 100th year celebration.

The celebration was a re-enactment of the first run to Wauwatosa in a locomotive, under steam, with two cars of the 1850 type. Crew and passengers were in full costume. The Milwaukee's mixed choral club and the 55 piece Hiawatha band were on hand for the music program.

Upon its return to Milwaukee, the old-time train met a six-car train of newest equipment and both remained on public display throughout the day. The celebration was carried on in other cities throughout the system including dinners, speeches and newspaper ads thanking the people of various communities. All in all it was a masterpiece of community relations, doing much to enhance the Milwaukee Road as a good neighbor.

The next 25 years was not spectacular financially, but neither did the road slip back into bankruptcy. The ultimate modernization of the Hiawathas was completed with the addition of Super Domes in 1952, and system wide dieselization occurred in January, 1955.

Freight service had been improved substantially.

Each railroad has its own personality, and that personality is displayed in the types of buildings, roadway structures and the like. The depot at Channing, Michigan (a division point) displays part of the Milwaukee character.

Passenger service is now operated by Amtrak with another whole new era making progress, albeit without Super Dome Hiawathas and Sky-top parlor cars.

The road has developed a research section for further traffic development and has, in recent years, expanded its territory to Oregon and Kentucky — two facets of railroading not enjoyed by all railroads in the 1970's.

The Milwaukee Road was a pioneer in the area of sales and traffic research. Most railroads had developed research departments, primarily in motive power, materials used in car construction, track and roadbed and fuel usage. As important as these areas are — and they are not to be neglected — very few companies took a look at their traffic developments, mix, and variations from month to month that could be caused by seasonal fluctuations or dissatisfaction of the shipper. However, in the early 1960's, the Milwaukee Road sought to correct this problem by the establishment of a Traffic Research Department.

The system developed by this department answered many questions, among them what is the profit earned on a carload? What type of traffic should be solicited? What rate adjustments need to be made?

There were three very important benefits for the railroad with this new traffic reporting system: a better sales service to shippers; a more productive use of salesmen's time, and a faster and more intelligent consideration of rate adjustment proposals. The reporting covers carloads terminated as well as originated, and is based on accounting data rather than car movement records, and shows total revenue produced by each individual carload as well as the Milwaukee's share of that revenue.

The reporting system was based on the four types of traffic: local movements, interline received, interline forwarded and bridge traffic. These were further broken down into (1) an Originating Commodity Report showing the details of carloads originated by station, state and patron.

(2) An Agency Summary report showing by commodities the total business originating and terminating in each of the company's sales territories.

(3) A Commodity Summary report showing for the system as a whole total carloads of each commodity for the month and year to date.

(4) An Originating and Terminating Summary, which shows total carloads of all commodities originated and terminated in each sales territory.

(5) A Patron Summary showing carloads originated by or delivered to each individual shipper.

This reporting system was a great asset not only to the Traffic Department, but also to the Operating Department who used it to adjust schedules for a greater accommodation of shippers.

The original idea of the Traffic Research Department was simply for traffic reporting, but the data led to other types of activities. For example, marketing research, cost analysis and operating costs, and finally even some freight train scheduling. The Department was heavily involved in the setting up of the new fast 55 hour train schedules between Chicago and the Pacific Northwest.

The original Traffic Research Department was eventually expanded and brought under the wings of the Market Development and Pricing section of the Traffic Department. In Market Development and Pricing there is now a Pricing and a Marketing Research section for each of the four commodity profit centers including a separate Economics and Cost Analysis Department. All of this has grown from one very small department, an offshoot of the Traffic Department, which consisted of only seven men in 1963. (This writer was a member of the seven-man team at that time.) One might say that this is a typical example of the Milwaukee Road's interest in research as a means of improving the company.

Few railroads in the United States have the potential and geographic position of the Milwaukee Road. It has been known as a company that could not leave things just as they are. Usually, this has brought many benefits to the company but

Switch stands, too, display the company personality. The Milwaukee can be identified by the striped targets. This photo was taken at the south end of the Channing yard.

The Milwaukee Road operates shops at Milwaukee, Wisconsin and for many years constructed large numbers of freight cars at these facilities. They became famous for the rib side cars. In 1977, new equipment is no longer constructed, but extensive rebuilding takes place. In fact, the rebuilding is so complete that for all practical purposes new equipment is still being constructed. (The Milwaukee Road)

there is also an element of conservatism, too. Ever since 1900, even with the Pacific Extension, the Milwaukee has not been content to be totally satisfied with its map or territory.

On August 6, 1970, the Road began serving Billings, Montana, as a condition of the Burlington Northern merger. Actual access to that city is by means of a car handling agreement with Burlington Northern through interchange points north, east and west of that commercial and distribution center.

March 22, 1971, the first CMStP&P train, operating over BN rails arrived in Portland, affording the Rose City additional single-line service to the Midwest and enabling Milwaukee Road participation in north-south traffic parallel to the Pacific Coast.

As a result of the Louisville and Nashville and Monon Railroad merger, the orange and black diesel of the Milwaukee began entering Louisville, Kentucky on March 1, 1973 by means of trackage rights from Bedford, Indiana over the Monon Division of the Family Lines member. Terminal facilities in the Falls City are provided by the Kentucky and Indiana Terminal Railroad.

The result is that the Milwaukee now serves a wider geographical area than ever before in its history.

Chapter 2
Passenger Trains

As mentioned in Chapter 1, the Milwaukee Road had an independent nature, and part of that nature was to put its best foot forward in the area of passenger service. It can be said that the Milwaukee Road outdid every other railroad in the United States in passenger train services. By the end of World War II, the company was virtually completely streamlined on all trains, with the exception of air conditioned sleepers, dining, diner lounge, parlor and cafe parlor cars of the standard heavy-weight type. It is also true that the commuter services were not streamlined and air conditioned, but that was true of every railroad; and even there, the Milwaukee Road would be eventually operating a superb and modern service. No other railroad could boast of the equipment and operating record of the Milwaukee Road, when even the Boy Scout specials were equipped with air conditioned streamlined coaches.

It would not be impossible to write an entire history of Milwaukee Road passenger service, but that is not the purpose of this book or even this chapter. The purpose here is to look at the non-Hiawatha service, and the various types of innovations put together by the Milwaukee in promoting its passenger service. The first part of the chapter will cover some of these innovations, while the second part will cover some of the famous trains operated over the Lines East.

During the mid-1920's, the Milwaukee Road began to feel the pinch of the competition from the private automobile. It did not take long for the company to begin to look at ways to provide suitable service and at the same time reduce costs.

We might pause here for a moment to look at a situation that the Milwaukee tried to deal with in a positive way. The railroads had been tied by government restrictions of all sorts, and were not able to change prices (fares and freight rates) or the product offered for changing market conditions. Consequently, the railroads had but one way to combat inflation and other problems (since it always took the ICC so long to rule on any change in service or rates) and that was to reduce costs. The condition, in effect, ruined the positive actions or thoughts of railroad managers and this eventually led to the conditions we have today in our railroad industry. It can be said that the Milwaukee made every effort to view service changes positively rather than negatively, and they did this despite two serious bankruptcies since 1920.

Such was the case of the passenger service on the Sturtevant-Racine, Wisconsin branch in 1925. The Milwaukee's main line misses the city of Racine, but they did not give up on the lucrative traffic that could be secured from that major city served directly by the Chicago & North Western. The expenses of the passenger train service offered on the branch became overly burdensome, and the road replaced the service with buses. Seven trips daily in each direction provided passenger, mail and express service connecting with mainline trains. The buses were 24 passenger inter-city vehicles and included a mail, baggage and express compartment at the rear. The buses were operated by railroad employees and tied up over night in a rented garage in Racine. Repairs were made by the company shops in Milwaukee.

Another innovation at the same time, was the testing of a diesel rail car. The company had been operating gas-electrics over various parts of the system for quite some time, but it pioneered the use of diesel power for passenger service. Now this is interesting, especially when viewed from the decision to use streamlined steam on the Hiawathas. In October, 1927, the company placed in service for test purposes between Monticello, Iowa and Calmar, what was probably the first all-American diesel electric rail car ever used in the U.S.A. The power plant was a six cylindar diesel engine built by the Foos Gas Engine Company of Springfield, Ohio, connected to a General Electric generator which furnished current for the two driving motors mounted on the front truck. The car was one built for the Milwaukee in 1912 and originally contained an eight cylinder gasoline engine.

The car made a daily 300 mile round trip between Monticello and Calmar involving a total of 32 stops and burning fuel at a rate of 5.26 miles per

Looking almost like a Hiawatha, train 28 races by Roundout with 7 cars at 80 miles per hour. No. 28 was an 80-minute train between Milwaukee and Chicago handling a parlor car, dining car and coaches. The schedule was a noon departure just 24 minutes ahead of the Olympian Hiawatha in 1951. (George Paterson Collection)

gallon. (Indeed! The author's own brother owned an automobile that did not achieve such mileage!) When handling a trailer car (weight about 33 tons), the fuel efficiency dropped to about 3.6 miles per gallon. In actual running, according to the July 7, 1928 issue of Railway Age, it was found to be possible to shut down the diesel engine when coasting on hills or into stations and while standing at stations, which materially added to the economy of the operation. Moreover, vibration was eliminated when the car was at rest.

During the late 1920's the declining passenger traffic continued to plague the Milwaukee. A careful study was made of the situation, and cost reductions were produced by the substitution of gas-electric cars, mixed trains and buses. This reduced steam passenger train mileage by 7,258 miles per day, according to the December 15, 1928 issue of Railway Age.

In 1929, the Milwaukee operated 10,891 miles of line. Of this, the main line from Chicago to Seattle comprised 2,189 miles, Chicago to Omaha, 487 miles and from Savanna, Illinois to Kansas City, 365 miles. The total primary main line mileage was 3,041 miles with 7,850 miles of secondary main lines and branch line territory. With such a large proportion of branch line mileage, the Milwaukee was one of the first railroads in the U.S.A. to give consideration to adjusting operations to meet the declining traffic mentioned earlier. As early as 1912, the company purchased a fleet of 70 foot gas-electrics in an effort to cope with the situation.

For the Milwaukee, there was no single solution. Each branch line or secondary main line had to be studied individually.

By 1928, the company was using motor coach (bus) as substitutes for steam passenger trains for

Train No. 10 en route from Milwaukee to Chicago rolls through Roundout, Illinois on July 31, 1947, with 7 cars at 65 miles per hour. (George-Paterson Collection)

distances under 20 miles. On the other hand, mixed train and gas-electric runs varied in length from about 12 miles to over 142 miles.

According to the December 15, 1928 issue of Railway Age, the Milwaukee substituted mixed train service in 25 different situations. This eliminated 66 passenger trains which operated 2,651.6 miles daily. In most cases the service supplemented one passenger train in each direction daily, but there was at least one case where the company substituted three mixed trains for three passenger trains on a 12.7 mile run in Iowa.

In every situation where a mixed train was run instead of a full passenger train, the revenue derived from the latter had decreased to such an extent as to be practically nil.

The permission to substitute mixed train service was not easy to obtain. Even though the company had informed the citizens of the communities affected, and there was little or no objections from them, the various state regulatory commissions took a dim view of the substitutions. Often the only point that permitted the commissions to change their minds was the fact that freight service would be improved with the faster schedule of the mixed train.

The average single trip of the mixed trains in 1928 was 44.7 miles. The longest distance run of any trip was 142.3 miles in South Dakota.

In 1928, the company operated 19 rail motor cars supplemented by 16 trailers, and by this time had had 16 years of experience with such equipment. Some operated on branches only, while others operated a combination main line-branch service, and still others were confined to main line duties only in local train service. The trips ranged from 61.3 miles to 341.2 miles.

The Milwaukee continued to use these methods to improve the passenger train operations, and by 1929 the company owned 5 of its own buses. They proudly displayed *The Milwaukee Road* on the sides, and were operated directly by the company, without a subsidiary, such as other railroad companies had set up during that time.

This method of improving passenger services was not the only type of improvement the company carried out. In the year 1935, we have the immortal Hiawathas placed in service between Chicago and Minneapolis. In 1937, the Chippewa went into service. Other improvements included the rebuilding of the Minneapolis depot, which was used not only by the Milwaukee Road, but also the Soo Line, Wisconsin Central and Rock Island Railroads.

Train 29 departs Milwaukee for Madison with No. 4 doing the honors. 29 connected with the Afternoon Hi and provided fast train service via Watertown daily except Saturday and Sunday. (Russ Porter)

World War II brought about unprecedented demands on the Milwaukee's passenger services. Up to eight troop trains were operated in each direction on the main line each day. During the war, loaded movements going west with empty trains returned east for more troops. After the war, came the more pleasant task of bringing home the troops, with the loaded trains moving east and the empties traveling west to Seattle and Tacoma. Troop trains were also interchanged with the Spokane, Portland & Seattle at Spokane, about the only time the Milwaukee Road actually participated in passenger movements of any kind between itself and that company.

After the war, the company began rebuilding the passenger car fleet and added new cars. As of November 1, 1947, the company had on order the following cars:

    28 sleepers
    56 coaches
    20 baggage cars
    10 dining cars
    19 mail cars
    22 lounge, parlor and combination type
        equipment

All except the first class sleepers were on order from the company shops. The Touralux cars were to be built by the Milwaukee Road while first class were being constructed by Pullman-Standard.

There were some unusual services offered by the passenger traffic department right after the war. Take, for example, the ski sleeper service. A sleeping car from Chicago to one of the several ski resorts was available to ski fans for weekend trips. Depending upon the weather and snow conditions, the road each week chose the best area from among the various resorts at Wausau, LaCrosse in Wisconsin and Houghton and Iron Mountain in Michigan. The car departed Chicago at 7:40 P.M. each Friday and returned to Chicago at 6:50 A.M. on the following Monday.

Another passenger service innovation was the "Fisherman," a summer train operating out of Chicago during its last years on Friday nights to Tomahawk, Minocqua and Woodruff, Wisconsin. Returning on Sunday nights, the train carried sleeping cars, dining car, lounge car and day coaches and operated through the summer to Labor Day weekend. This train operated in 1926, '28, '29, 1931 through 1942; and finally 1946, '47 and '48. During the 20's and 1934, it operated daily, other seasons were weekends only.

It is interesting to note that despite the fact that the Milwaukee experimented with diesel rail cars in the late 1920's, and operated an extensive gas-electric fleet, it never purchased a Budd Company Rail Diesel Car. Instead, the final curtain on such equipment was drawn when the railroad built two diesel rail cars in 1948 with 1000 hp diesel electric power plants. The two unique models were constructed at, you guessed it, the Milwaukee Road's own shops and were capable of handling 4 cars and could operate up to a maximum speed of 75 miles per hour. The front end of the cars resembled a modern diesel locomotive, while the rear of the cars contained a 41½ foot baggage room. The two cars, 5900 and 5901, were 85 feet long. The cars operated over several routes, and one was operated for a time between Harlowton and Great Falls, Montana.

1950 brought a new sales campaign, which included a booklet entitled, "Let the Engineer Do the Driving." The booklet included a whole series of cartoons aimed at the harassed driver, and was designed to convince him that next time, he should take the Milwaukee Road.

1950 still found the Milwaukee Road operating a number of its sleepers. Although in 1927, the company had signed a contract with Pullman to oper-

The eastbound Olympian pauses at Montevideo, Minnesota on the main line from the west coast. It is May, 1927 and the size of the train reflects the good business enjoyed before the depression. (Harold K. Vollrath Collection)

ate some sleepers on some trains, the road continued its independent sleeper services, and many trains carried both a Pullman conductor and Milwaukee Road sleeping car conductor, as well as a train conductor. The Columbian was such an example.

There were many other innovations by the Milwaukee Road's passenger services. For example, their passenger car truck has never been excelled by another passenger car truck for riding qualities. This writer cannot understand why other companies have not studied the Milwaukee Road's superb truck.

Still another innovation was the book type coupon passenger ticket. Measuring 3¼ by 6¼ inches, the book contained in order, an agent's stub, six ticket coupons and a passenger's receipt coupon. All inner pages had a carbon backing so that the selling agent only had to fill in the agent's stub, make one punch of any necessary endorsements and make a single validation stamp to execute the entire ticket. The purpose of the new form was greater convenience to passengers, easier honoring by conductors and simplified issuance by agents. The ticket was devised by the Western Lines Committee for Simplification of Ticket forms, but was placed in experimental service on the Milwaukee Road.

All of these things added up to a fine train service offered by a very reliable railroad company. Many of the trains, in addition to the world-famous Hiawathas, literally became as famous as the Broadway Limited and the Super Chief.

The Pioneer Limited

The Pioneer Limited's heritage goes back to 1872 when trains 1 and 4 were listed in the timetables for through overnight travel (21 hours, 10 minutes) between Chicago and the Twin Cities. It was not until 1898 that the train received its name "Pioneer Limited" with new equipment from Barney & Smith, and a 13-hour schedule. The train apparently received a gradual, but thorough re-equipping during the years 1905 through 1908. By 1914, the train was re-equipped again and ran daily in two sections. The first section carried the head-end cars and coaches, while the second section was "the only solid sleeping car train from Chicago to St. Paul — Minneapolis" by the road's own admission.

But the finest Pioneer Limited was to come in 1927. On May 21st of that year, the Milwaukee Road placed in service new equipment that was completely roller-bearing equipped. Another feature of the easy-riding cars was the use of rubber cushions between truck center plates and truck bolsters, and in the equalized spring caps. As a safety measure, car bodies and trucks were locked together.

The entire train including at least one locomotive, F-3 Pacific No. 6109, was decorated in the Milwaukee Road orange with dark maroon trimmings. The interior of each sleeper was of Spanish design and coloring, with walls, ceilings, lighting fixtures, furnishings and all other details planned to produce harmony and beauty of architectural line and decorative effect. The general use of candelabra to the exclusion of ceiling dome lights wherever possible was in innovation which promoted the artistic and homelike atmosphere. The tunnel-like effect in the open sleeping cars was relieved by a series of arches of Spanish outline across the aisle and connecting the headboards.

The library club car was finished in mahogany with furnishings in harmony with the rest of the train. The carpet was a rich red with large floral design and chairs and sofas were upholstered in brown Spanish leather. Service to both clubrooms was provided from a well equipped buffet in the center of the car. In addition to numerous armchairs, two sofas and four sets of section seats for card players, each club room had a writing desk and movable oval table. The beamed ceiling of the library club car was ivory tinted, lined in gold. The lighting system consisted of snowball ceiling fix-

tures and side bracket lights of similar design. The use of tapestry panels in place of mirrors for decorative purposes was a new feature.

The dining car had a capacity of 36 passengers and was finished in the light brown mahogany with beamed ceilings as in the library club car. The straight back chairs with spring cushion leather seats had cream colored slips with figured design, while the du Pont Fabricoid window shades, furnished by the O'Fallon Railway Supply Company were of a mottled maroon and silver.

Another innovation was the electrical refrigeration, which avoided the necessity of stops for icing.

The compartment drawing room cars were identical in design and furnishings with the other sleeping cars, except that the upholstery color scheme of the rooms was in alternating blue and tan. The rooms, not only in this car, but in drawing rooms and compartments of the open sleeping cars, had bronze reading lamps with mica shades. A reading lamp was also provided at the sofa in the drawing rooms in addition to the section lamps. Other special features included a clock in each room, with a small electric night lamp above it, electric fans and individual heat control, a shoe servidor accessible from the inside as well as from the corridor, so that shoes could be removed for cleaning without distrubing passengers, a small door knocker instead of a buzzer, and a cabinet for toilet articles.

The single-bedroom observation car contained six individual bedrooms, each room being designed for one-person occupancy having a bed with deep box spring, thick comfortable mattress and silk spread. The women's lounge of this car was very roomy with four comfortable arm chairs, console table, mirror and completely equipped dressing room, finished in dull ivory enamel. The Spanish motif of color and design was again carried out in the parlor which contained a four-foot writing desk facing the windows at one side and provided with a writing lamp, a library table and magazine rack on the opposite side. The seating arrangement was unusual in that six large and comfortable chairs were provided in addition to the usual armchairs and couches. Bronze side bracket wall candelabra add to the beauty of the room. The recessed and semi-enclosed observation platform, with brass capped railing and gates, had steps on one side only.

This equipment rolled on the Pioneer Limited until after World War II, when the train was again re-equipped with the finest of streamlined equipment.

Interior of coach showing the old non-reclining seats in service on the Olympian in pre-Hiawatha days. (The Milwaukee Road)

Train 20, the Varsity, to Chicago pauses at Janesville, Wisconsin in 1950. The Varsity, with the Sioux, provided double daily service between Chicago and Madison with cafe parlor car service. The baggage cars in the background were set out cars for mail and express service. (Harold K. Vollrath Collection)

The 1948 edition of the Pioneer Limited was a magnificent train. Diesel powered, the train consisted of a varied amount of head-end cars (up to six), three coaches, a Tip Top Tap Diner (complete with mid-night snacks, hot sandwiches and hot soup), two 8 duplex roomette, 6 roomette, 4 double bedroom cars between Minneapolis and Chicago, one 8-6-4 car between Minneapolis and Milwaukee and still another between St. Paul and Chicago. There were also two 16 duplex roomettes, 4 double bedroom cars between Minneapolis and Chicago. The train was very heavy on sleeper space with six regularly assigned cars to and from the Twin Cities.

These were not the only sleepers handled by 1 and 4. Northbound, No. 1 handled two 8 section, 2 compartment and 1 drawing room sleeping cars for Tomahawk to Minocqua-Woodruff. One originated in Chicago, while the other was added in Milwaukee. There was also a through Chicago-Woodruff coach as well as head-end cars. This meant that No. 1 had a consist of 8 sleepers out of Milwaukee. Southbound No. 4 did not handle the Woodruff cars, as they were switched into the Fast Mail, No. 56 at New Lisbon.

However, No. 4 did handle the through sleepers off of the Copper Country Limited from Milwaukee to Chicago. This included a through 10 section, 1 compartment, 1 drawing room car from Calumet from the Duluth, South Shore & Atlantic Railway (now the Soo Line) and a through 10 section, 2 compartment car from Sault Ste. Marie off the Soo Line's Atlantic Limited at Pembine.

By 1955, the sleeping car traffic on the Pioneer Limited had declined to a point where it was necessary to run only two Chicago-Minneapolis cars, one Chicago-St. Paul and one Milwaukee-Minneapolis — still heavy when compared to other trains, but definitely less than five years previous. There were a few differences with the connection sleepers off the Tomahawk and Copper Country. The Sault Ste. Marie car was tri-weekly, while the Woodruff car ran in No. 4 southbound into Chicago having been handled in No. 56 from New Lisbon to Milwaukee. The Milwaukee set out to and from Woodruff had been discontinued.

The Pioneer Limited Sleeping car runs, however, were now to stabilize for almost the next 10 years. The four sleeper runs did not change until after the mid-1960's. Meanwhile, by 1957 the Pioneer operated in a new dress of armour yellow and Harbor Mist Grey, a la Union Pacific although there were some slight modifications. The Milwaukee Road's application was somewhat different from the UP's, with a thinner stripe at the top of the car. Nevertheless, the new scheme fit the

One of the leaders of the fleet, the Pioneer Limited poses on the "wrong main" against the current of traffic. Long trains such as this caused the Milwaukee to design the first 4-6-4's. (The Milwaukee Road)

Pioneer Limited quite well. Also by this time, the diner lounges were a pair of "Grove" diner-parlors, built in 1948, which had their parlor seats replaced by a lounge.

After the mid-1960's, the train began to feel the pinch of the private automobile and businessman trade went to the airlines between Chicago and the Twin Cities. Finally with the loss of mail contracts, the train was running with but 2 or 3 head-end cars, 2 coaches, 1 diner lounge car and 1 sleeper between Chicago and Minneapolis. The diner lounge still provided the finest of Milwaukee Road midnight snacks and breakfast, and the quality of the service had not been allowed to suffer. However, the Pioneer Limited was discontinued because of the passenger losses in September, 1970 after 98 years of service to the traveling public.

The Copper Country Limited

The Copper Country Limited was also a train of long standing tradition (since 1907) for the Milwaukee Road and the Duluth, South Shore & Atlantic Railway. It provided overnight service to Michigan's Upper Peninsula from Chicago. It served ski areas, such as Iron Mountain and

Houghton, and carried through coaches as well as sleepers with a set out coach at Channing. For a good deal of its career, however, it did not offer dining car service on the northbound run, and was actually a train that could be called a "Maid of all Work."

During the early 1950's, she also carried a through Pullman for Sault Ste. Marie which had been in regular service since June 9, 1930, and a Beaver Tail parlor car that was set out at Milwaukee. Head-end equipment was always four or more cars including at least one Soo Line for the Sault Ste. Marie train at Pembine.

After October, 1951 the Southbound Copper Country was combined either with the Pioneer Limited or train 56 between Milwaukee and Chicago. Coach Passengers were required to change trains at Milwaukee, but sleeping cars were always a through operation.

By 1960, the Copper Country carried a lunch lounge car between Chicago and Milwaukee, as well as an 8 duplex roomette, 6 roomette, 4 double bedroom sleeping car. Head-end traffic had grown to as much as 8 cars, much of it for Milwaukee and Green Bay, including flexi-van cars for the latter point. North of Green Bay, trains 9 and 10 carried two or three head-end cars, two or three coaches and one sleeper as the normal consist. During the summers, however, the consist of the train often swelled to twice its normal size to accommodate campers and tourists for Michigan's northland. This consist persisted until the train was discontinued in early 1968.

The Columbian

The Columbian was the secondary passenger train between Chicago and Seattle-Tacoma. She was placed in service on May 29, 1911, and continued until 1931. She was reinstated in June, 1947. She could be called "The Maid of all Work," for she performed all of the heavy head-end work and local stops for much of the distance. During the early 1950's, the train consist of five to six head-end cars, dormitory coach, one or two coaches, one through Chicago-Tacoma 6 section, 6 double bedroom car, one Chicago-Minneapolis 10 sec, 1 drawing room, 1 compartment, one 14 section tourist sleeper between Chicago and Tacoma, and one diner lounge car for the entire distance. The tourist sleeper was operated by the Milwaukee Road, while the first class sleepers were operated by Pullman.

The classic open section sleeper was a fine way to travel in 1927 when these roller bearing beauties were built. (The Milwaukee Road)

Parlor car accommodations were offered on the Pioneer during the late 1920's prior to the speeding up of the train between Chicago and Minneapolis. An early evening departure from Chicago, parlor cars with their soft single seating, provided Chicago — Milwaukee passengers with first class comfort. (The Milwaukee Road)

The earliest bedrooms actually had one single bed (similar to European first class sleepers). Soon this type was replaced on all railroads by sofa type beds which could be used as day accommodations. This photo shows the door open between two adjoining rooms to make a suite. This style had no upper berth. Only the finest accommodations were offered on the Pioneer Limited. (The Milwaukee Road)

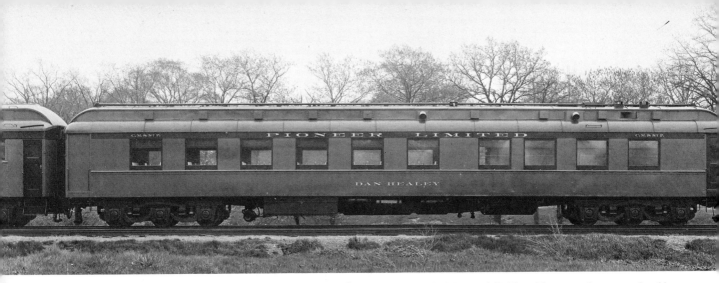

The dining car "Dan Healey" was one of two such cars operated on the Pioneer Limited. Dan Healey was the well-known dining car steward who could remember passengers by name, and knew their likes and dislikes. He was a fine example of how passenger train crews should treat their passengers. (The Milwaukee Road)

The train operated an overnight Chicago-Minneapolis run, and No. 17 hit Mobridge about 4:30 P.M. the next afternoon. Eastbound 18 departed Mobridge about 1:50 P.M. with an overnight run from Minneapolis to the Windy City, arriving there about 8:45 A.M.

As the 1950's progressed, the train fell victim to the automobile, and was cut back to Ortonville in February, 1957 and discontinued completely in March, 1957. From that time on, the Olympian Hiawatha was to go it alone to the coast, but by the 1960's, the Olympian too would be cut back until it was nothing more than a Minneapolis-Aberdeen train. History repeats itself again and again, only in different ways.

The Southwest Limited

The Southwest Limited served the Milwaukee-Chicago-Kansas City run, and did this despite severe competition from the Santa Fe. The height of its career was during the late 1920's. (See THE MILWAUKEE railROADer, October, 1973 issue). Train 25 consisted of several head-end cars, three or four coaches, dining car, one 8 section, 1 drawing room, 2 compartment sleeper, one 10 section, 1 drawing room, 2 compartment sleeper and one observation sleeper lounge. The train departed Chicago's Union Station at 6:00 P.M. At 5:00 P.M., the Wisconsin section of the train departed Milwaukee with head-end equipment, coaches, dining car and 12 section, 1 drawing room sleepers — one for

Dining car service was not the only extra provided by the Pioneer, but also a new club car went into service about 1928. (The Milwaukee Road)

Interior views of the "Hennepin". (The Milwaukee Road)

Omaha and one for Kansas City. Still another sleeper operated a Davenport-Milwaukee run. The two sections were consolidated at Savanna, Illinois and operated into Kansas City with a substantial train of well over 12 to 15 cars including 6 sleepers. This included cars from Cedar Rapids, which were switched in Ottumwa.

The depression, automobile, new air service and the faster trains of the Santa Fe brought the train's demise. The train was eventually combined with the Arrow between Chicago and Savanna, which was actually a good move. By 1951, the Milwaukee still operated through sleepers between Milwaukee-Chicago-Kansas City, but were of the heavy weight type. Dining car service was discontinued west of Savanna. By 1955 the name was dropped as well as sleeping car service. In 1958, the train was cut back to a Milwaukee-Savanna service and in 1965, the train was taken off altogether.

The Sioux

Now here was an interesting train, which began service June, 1926. This was the Chicago-Rapid City, South Dakota train via Madison, Canton, Sioux Falls, and Mitchell. The train ran on a 28 hour schedule westbound in the early 1950's and included a through Chicago-Rapid City 10 section, 1 compartment, 1 drawing room Milwaukee Road sleeper. The train departed Chicago at 9:30 P.M. and arrived the next night at 12:40 A.M. The sleeper was then set for occupancy until 8:00 A.M. The train also carried an 8 section, 2 compartment, 1 drawing room sleeper between Chicago and Mason City, also a Milwaukee Road Car. A Pullman 8-2-1 car ran between Chicago and Austin,

Minnesota. Through coaches were operated between all points. Eastbound the Rapid City service was operated via Sioux Falls to Chicago on the Mid-west Hiawatha.

The eastbound Sioux also originated in Sioux Falls and carried Milwaukee Road sleepers from that point and Mason City, as well as a parlor car and dining car from Madison to Chicago. No. 22 departed Sioux Falls at 4:10 P.M. and operated via Canton to Madison. Arriving there at about 6:30

During the streamlined era, the Pioneer Limited carried a single car offering both dining car and lounge car services. With the kitchen in the middle, one end contained the dining room with 6 tables for 4 passengers each, while the opposite end contained the tavern section. These cars served superb midnight snacks and breakfasts for the approximately 11 p.m. to 7 a.m. run. (The Milwaukee Road)

A big "Northern" powers train 108, the Arrow, by the Bensenville station en route to Chicago from Omaha and Kansas City. This overnight accommodation run was similar to the Pioneer during the standard era. (The Milwaukee Road)

A.M., the train picked up additional equipment and arrived in Chicago at 9:30 A.M., providing a morning service from Madison. The train also carried the Austin Pullman service. Trains 11 and 22 will long be remembered because of the switching that was performed on the train all along the entire route. Few trains on the Milwaukee were pulled apart and put back together as much as this train was.

The train finished her long distance career as a Chicago-Canton, South Dakota train via Madison, having been cut back from Sioux Falls to Canton October 1, 1951. She operated over the famous pontoon bridge over the Mississippi River at Prairie du Chien, Wisconsin. She continued to carry a Chicago-Mason City sleeper service in the mid-1950's. The Sioux was cut back to a Chicago-Madison service in 1960.

The Chicago-Madison service was a twice daily operation with the Varsity. The Sioux operated from Madison to Chicago in the morning, returning in the evening. She carried one head-end car, sometimes more, two or more coaches and a cafe parlor car. During the mid-1960's, a Super Dome operated between Chicago and Madison. The Varsity operated opposite the Sioux, and thus provided a twice daily operation in both directions between

Chicago and the capital city of Wisconsin. The cafe parlor car service was discontinued on both sets of trains in early 1965. In 1968, the Varsity was cut back to a Friday, Saturday and Sunday operation only. The entire operation was discontinued on May 1, 1971 — Amtrak day.

The Arrow

For many years, the Arrow was the Milwaukee's fleet leader between Chicago and Omaha, as well as Sioux Falls, South Dakota. Providing full sleeping, dining car and observation lounge service, the train operated on an overnight schedule between Chicago and Omaha and South Dakota points. The Dakota section was switched in or out of the main line train at Manila, Iowa.

The train offered a superb service to residents along the Milwaukee's main line, a main line that had to compete with the "City" streamliners of the Chicago & North Western. Nevertheless the Arrow was operated with traditional Milwaukee finesse.

The status of the Arrow was to change significantly when the Union Pacific transferred its streamliners to the Milwaukee Road. For two years after the acquisition of the city trains, a Lake series 10-6 sleeper was operated between Chicago and Omaha, and then a 6 roomette, 8 duplex roomette and 4 bedroom car until fall, 1958. During this time a 16 duplex roomette, 4 bedroom operated to Sioux Falls, otherwise the train continued to carry on as a "Maid of all Work." This sometimes expanded the train's consist to as much as 30 cars. Such an example could be found every so often in the mid-1960's. After discontinuance of the Omaha Sleepers, the train normally carried one sleeper (16 duplex roomette, 4 double bedroom) from Sioux Falls, to three coaches, one lunch lounge car and four head-end cars. However, perishables from the West Coast shipped by Railway Express, were often coupled to the rear end — as many as 20 REA Express refers — with a rider coach. What an impressive train!

Gradually though, the train diminished in importance, and she was discontinued in 1967.

Other Passenger Trains

The Milwaukee Road operated a variety of other services, some of which have become quite famous over the years. The Fast Mail, trains 57 and 56, operated overnight, every night between Chicago and Minneapolis. The mail did not carry passengers west bound, but did provide a rider coach on the east-bound run. In the early 1950's and prior to that time, she carried a 10 section, 1 drawing room, 1 compartment sleeper as well as the coach. Passengers had a choice of three overnight trains to Chicago on the Milwaukee, the Pioneer Limited Fast Mail and Columbian. Train 56 also carried the Woodruff cars either to Milwaukee or Chicago from New Lisbon. The length of this train varied from never less than a dozen to nearly 30 and included up to four Rail Post Office cars. The train was discontinued in late April, 1971.

The company has operated a corridor service between Chicago and Milwaukee, and this has always been a high speed service. A variety of services were offered including parlor cars, dining and lounge cars, and even Super Domes on trains that were not Hiawathas or the Pioneer Limited.

And finally, the Milwaukee operated a group of trains that have been written about countless times before, including by this author: the Union Pacific streamliners and domeliners between Chicago and Council Bluffs, Iowa. Originally there were five streamliners in each direction daily. The shift from the C&NW to the Milwaukee Road was made on October 30, 1955, and became known as Union Pacific day on the Milwaukee. The result of the transfer prompted the Milwaukee to repaint all of its passenger equipment in Union Pacific

yellow, with the exception of the commutation equipment.

The most unusual of the Milwaukee Road's passenger service was provided by trains 101 and 104 between Fayette and Terre Haute. This pair of trains operated for the benefit of miners. Train 101 departed Maple Avenue in Terre Haute, Indiana at 5:55 A.M. with a 6:07 A.M. arrival in Fayette, just six miles away. Returning, 104 got out of Fayette at 3:02 P.M. with a 3:10 P.M. arrival at the Maple Avenue station. This service was discontinued by 1953. The above schedules were in effect in the early 1950's and were the last remnants of a passenger service on the old Chicago, Terre Haute and South Eastern that extended from West Dana to Westport.

Very few railroads operated passenger service the way the Milwaukee Road did. Not only in quantity, but in variety. What other road operated a fleet of streamliners like the Hiawathas, along with Super Domes, short domes on the UP trains, dining cars with midnight snacks, ski trains to Iron Mountain and elsewhere, tour trains to Wisconsin Dells using commutation equipment on Sundays, and streamlined coaches on all trains, *all trains* by 1950! The Milwaukee Road is to be commended for the service it provided the American traveling public.

What appears to be train 23, an 85-minute train to Milwaukee, departs the Windy City with the skyline of Chicago on the right as a commuter train backs to the Union Station. The reader should note that the Milwaukee Road actually had joint trackage with the Pennsylvania Railroad into the Union Depot. Note the PRR type signal above the big Hudson powering the seven car train. It is significant, too, that it is 1949 and virtually all Milwaukee main line operations were streamlined and air conditioned. No other railroad could make that claim. (Harold K. Vollrath Collection)

For a number of years the Milwaukee operated a gas-electric between Racine, Wisconsin and Sturtevant to connect with main line services. In 1926 the company replaced the service with a bus.

Most motor car trains were generally unimaginative and purely functional. Not so on the Milwaukee Road. Feast your eyes on this open-end wood coach observation car with stained glass and the whole works. It is July, 1939 and motor 3820 is handling trailer car 5925 on a local out of Marquette, Iowa. This is an old Dubuque Division train. (Harold K. Vollrath Collection)

Motor car 5934 was photographed at Milwaukee in September, 1949. The Milwaukee Road went to great efforts to provide efficient and reliable operation of all passenger service — even the branch line locals. Note that the car has been equipped with roller bearing trucks. (Harold K. Vollrath Collection)

Orange and maroon motor 5933 handles a wooden coach at Mason City, Iowa. (W. S. Kuba Collection)

With the Mid-west Hiawatha in the background, motor 5932 heads up still another Hiawatha type coach for connecting service between Madrid and Des Moines. It is August, 1951 and the "Road" still operated a connecting train for the Midwest Hi, and one should take notice that the Milwaukee provided an air conditioned streamlined coach. (Harold K. Vollrath Collection)

Some of the early gas-electrics were constructed with bullet noses. This is the 5903 photographed in 1941. (W. S. Kuba Collection)

Mixed trains were also prevalent on the Milwaukee. This is train 21 departing Janesville, Wisconsin en route to Mineral Point. (Russ Porter)

Train 106, a mid-day Madison to Milwaukee runs, travels over the double track main line through Wauwatosa, Wisconsin on December 9, 1956. 106 was one of three daily trains from the Wisconsin Capitol to the beer center of the world. (Jim Scribbins)

With Fairbanks-Morse passenger power leading, train 118, the Varsity, departs Madison for Chicago with five cars including a cafe-parlor car. 118 was the evening departure to Chicago. (Russ Porter)

Train 107, the Challenger-Hiawatha passes the west edge of Marion, Iowa on its combined train routing of the Mid-west Hi to Omaha, and the Challenger to Los Angeles. (W. S. Kuba Collection)

Alco 14-B, with a rebuilt nose, arrives at Canton, South Dakota with train 11, the Sioux, en route from Chicago to Rapid City, South Dakota. (Jim Scribbins)

Train 55, sometimes known as the 2nd Mail, operated on a much more leisurely schedule between Chicago and Minneapolis. 55 is shown here arriving in the Twin Cities with deadhead sleepers on the head-end in August, 1957. (Jim Scribbins)

Train 108, the Challenger travels along the Fox River east of
Elgin on the last leg of its run to Chicago. The date is June 20,
1957 and not all Milwaukee units were repainted yellow and
grey. (Jim Scribbins)

Motor 5901 handled the Austin section of equipment that operated between Chicago and the Minnesota city. Trains 157 and
158 connected with main line trains at La Crosse and carried
the Austin sleeper. The train is shown here at Austin with a
mail and baggage, combine and sleeper. (Jime Scribbins)

The romance of the "Fast Mail" (trains 57 and 56) could not be
equalled anywhere. Running at night between Chicago and St.
Paul-Minneapolis, the drama was even more profound. Here 57
cools its wheels at the old Milwaukee station with a rear-end
brakeman compartment baggage car (rider car) and flexi-van
bringing up the rear. This photo was taken during the Christmas mail rush of 1959 by Jim Scribbins.

The Milwaukee Road utilized commuter equipment during off times for special trains, such as this Girl Scouts Special passing Pewaukee Lake with almost 1200 passengers. This particular train made two round trips between Milwaukee and Watertown on May 11, 1963 for the benefit of the scouts. (Jim Scribbins)

Train 26, the Savanna-Milwaukee local (the former Southwest Limited between Milwaukee-Kansas City), takes siding to meet time freight 75 at Delevan, Wisconsin. Train 75 was sometimes known as the beer train to the southwest. (Jim Scribbins)

During the 1960's, Sunday specials from Chicago and Milwaukee to Wisconsin Dells also utilized bi-level commuter equipment. Such a train is loading passengers at Milwaukee on July 7, 1963. Note the Fairbanks-Morse switcher in yellow at the right of the photo. (Jim Scribbins)

Train 46 was a late afternoon train from Milwaukee to Chicago providing coach service only. The tracks in the foreground belong to the Elgin, Joliet and Eastern Railway as this is the famed crossing with the rule to "Slow to 100 M.P.H." The old Chicago, North Shore & Milwaukee Electric line bridge is in the background. Not only is the North Shore missing but so is the depot on the left. (Russ Porter)

Train 12 was a noon departure from Milwaukee to Chicago, and on this Sunday in October, 1964, the company is balancing power and moving three GP-9's (208, 209 and 207) along with the 103 C and 100 B. A lot of power for just an 8 car train. (Jim Scribbins)

With the demise of the Olympian Hiawatha, Super Domes found themselves in Madison and Milwaukee trains. Here train 117 rolls toward Madison with a four car train in Nov. 1964. (Jim Scribbins)

Train 46 in June, 1966 rolls toward Chicago with a flexi-van, one Union Pacific coach, one Milwaukee Road coach and two baggage cars. UP coaches frequently traveled to Milwaukee. (William A. Raia)

Here we have train 12 again departing Milwaukee on a Sunday in January, 1966. Again commuter cars were being utilized, as long distance coaches were in short supply. With electric head-end power for lighting, heating, etc., the baggage cars had to be handled on the rear end. No. 12 provided coach service only, and usually ran with streamlined coaches except when they were required for other service. (Jim Scribbins)

Eastbound train 58 departs New Lisbon with eight cars in July, 1966. A daylight run from Minneapolis, the train was primarily head-end traffic. (A. Robert Johnson)

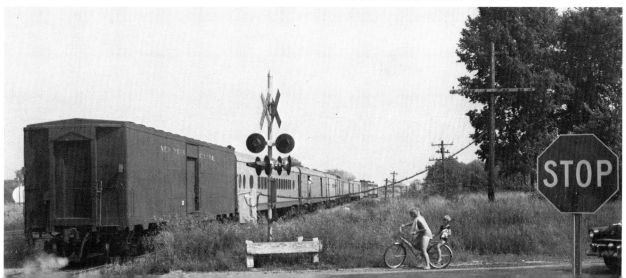

Train 2 passes 58 at New Lisbon, Wisconsin. At the time this photo was taken in 1966, the Milwaukee time tables indicated five first class trains in each direction daily. Ten years later Amtrak operated but two in each direction. (A. Robert Johnson)

In a little more than two years down the road, this train and hundreds of others would be dropped. This photo shows the City of Portland/Denver crossing the Des Plaines River on its way west with 9 cars on March 1, 1969. The lead unit, FP-45 No. 3, is the third Milwaukee engine to carry that number; the narrow gauge power mentioned in Chapter 1, the streamlined Atlantics and finally the FP-45's. (Jim Scribbins)

Another view of 58 at Sparta with 2 diesel units and 15 cars. Almost like a freight train. (Jim Scribbins)

This photo was taken during the last year of the Fast Mail. Train 57 is shown here at Milwaukee with former dormitory-baggage car 1351 serving as a rider car for the conductor and crew. Photo taken on August 12, 1970. Eight and one half more months, and the train would be replaced by the Burlington Northern's Pacific Zip. (Jim Scribbins)

It is 12:45 a.m. and the Vagabond Ski Club has returned to Milwaukee from Iron Mountain, Michigan for a week-end of skiing. At this late hour, the station is all but deserted. The seven car train arrived on time, a Milwaukee Road tradition even for passenger extras. (Jim Scribbins)

The last of what was once the Northwoods Hiawatha was simply a passenger extra running between New Lisbon and Wausaw, connecting with the Morning Hi after the Afternoon Hi had been discontinued. This train is eastbound approaching the Port Edward's depot on September 2, 1970. (Jim Scribbins)

A football special from Milwaukee to Madison races thru Wauwatosa on November 7, 1970. The 16 car train was powered by three FP units and demonstrated the Milwaukee's ability to handle large special movements. (Jim Scribbins)

Train 104, the combined "Cities" from the west coast makes its final trip to Chicago. The sad train makes its final stop at Marion, Iowa. An impressive train, she was powered by four Milwaukee passenger units but not accepted by Amtrak; she runs no more. (W. S. Kuba)

Only six more weeks, and the Milwaukee Road fleet will be no more. Train 12 departs Milwaukee on Sunday, March 21, 1971, the first day of spring. With coaches built for the 1948 Hiawathas, the train reflects the loss of mail and express contracts and the length is abbreviated from days gone by. (Jim Scribbins)

A little known operation was the interchange of mail cars between the Milwaukee Road and the New York Central in Chicago. This photo shows a switch crew about to depart the LaSalle Street Station Coach Yards with but one Railway Express Agency car. (Russ Porter)

With less than a month to go to Amtrak, train 22, the Sioux, comes off the Second Sub from Madison and glides onto the Chicago-Milwaukee line at Roundout on April 10, 1971. As of early 1977, passenger service between Chicago and Madison has still not been resumed. (Jim Scribbins)

The old Milwaukee Road depot in Milwaukee was an impressive depot and did not have the dingy appearance of many depots its age. This photo by Jim Scribbins shows the east end of the depot with a passenger GP-9 in the yellow and grey scheme poking its nose out in the sunshine.

The old Milwaukee depot as seen through Pere Marquette park. Photo taken in April, 1962. (Jim Scribbins)

The type F6a Hudsons were the result of extensive testing and this particular locomotive is actually lettered for the Chicago, Terre Haute and South Eastern. Note the sub lettering below the coal load. The 6416 is shown here at Milwaukee in September, 1936. (George-Paterson Collection)

This steam locomotive, type S-1, 4-8-4 Northern, was first tested in passenger service between Minneapolis and Harlowton. The tests resulted in the company purchasing 4-6-4's instead. Note the special platform built over the pilot for test purposes. (The Milwaukee Road)

The Hudsons were operated in passenger service between Minneapolis and Harlowton. This engine is shown in Minneapolis after renumbering in June, 1938. (George-Paterson Collection)

The S-2 Northerns were mainly for freight, but were assigned to the Olympian between Minneapolis and Harlowton. They could not operate east of Western Avenue in Chicago. (The Milwaukee Road)

The S-3 Northerns were built on Rock Island frames and carried a Union Pacific type tender. They regularly pulled trains 107 and 108, the Arrow, between Chicago and Omaha. (The Milwaukee Road)

This is famous No. 15, the diesel that demonstrated beyond a doubt that the passenger diesel was here to stay. (The Milwaukee Road)

The Milwaukee operated a number of GP-9's in passenger service, such as the 207 shown here in switching service for the Western Avenue coach yards in Chicago.

One of the most unique engines assigned to passenger service in any fashion was the Fairbanks-Morse diesel switcher No. 718 at Milwaukee. Painted in the yellow and grey color scheme, she was one of the most colorful switchers on the system. (Russ Porter)

Car 1978 was a former RPO-Baggage car modified for mail storage service. 75 feet long, the car once contained a 15 RPO section. Photographed at Milwaukee in August, 1964 by Jim Scribbins.

The next set of photos will show a variety of passenger equipment. Hiawatha equipment is included in this chapter because of their service in non-Hiawatha trains. The first photo shows car 1918, an 82-foot former sleeper rebuilt for mail storage, still retaining the air conditioning bubble in 1964. (Jim Scribbins)

Express car 1056, 75 feet long, was an insulated car built by ACF in 1928. Photographed in July, 1964. (Jim Scribbins)

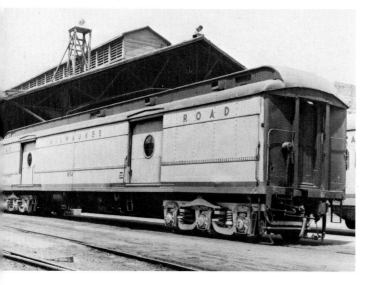

Express car 1074, 75 feet long, was built by the Milwaukee shops in 1928. Carrying the yellow and grey, the car was photographed in June, 1964 by Jim Scribbins.

Express car 1102 (Series 1100 to 1122) was 76 feet long and was one of the first streamlined baggage cars, constructed in 1935. (The Milwaukee Road)

Car 1336 is a 75-foot post-war express car built for general service including the Hiawathas, series 1317 to 1336. (The Milwaukee Road)

Storage car 2016 was rebuilt from either a touralux sleeper or a diner in 1964 at the Milwaukee shops. 85 feet long, the entire series ran from 2008 to 2017. (Jim Scribbins)

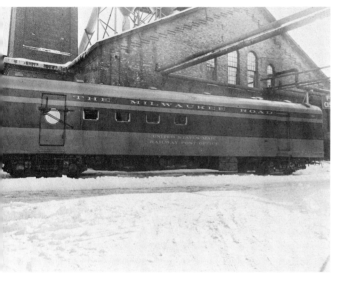

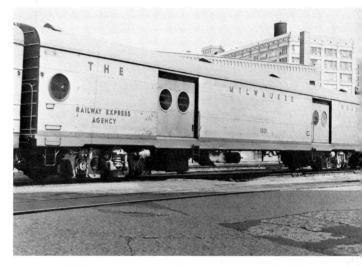

Full Rail Post Office car No. 2152 (and 2153) were built specifically for the Morning Hiawatha, but later served in other capacities. The 60-foot cars were classics. (The Milwaukee Road)

Express car 1331 contained a conductor's room at one end. Built in 1947 by the Milwaukee Shops, the car was photographed in August, 1964 by Jim Scribbins.

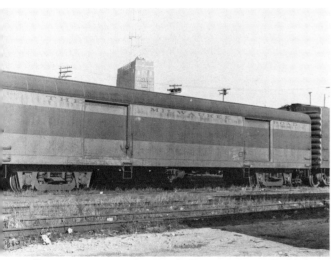

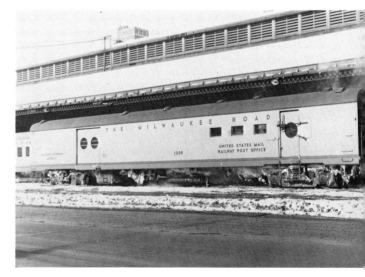

Storage car 2050 (66 feet over buffers) was a one-of-a-kind car. Photographed in 1965 by Jim Scribbins.

Mail and Express cars 1209 to 1229 were 75 feet long and contained a 30-foot RPO section. Photo taken in December, 1963 at Milwaukee. (Jim Scribbins)

60-foot cars 2150 and 2151 contained a full RPO and were built in 1938. Car 2150 was photographed in train 1, the Pioneer Limited in Milwaukee on October 15, 1965. (Jim Scribbins)

Coach 4440 was constructed in 1934 by the Company Shops. It is shown here in train 24, the Traveler, at the Milwaukee depot. (Jim Scribbins)

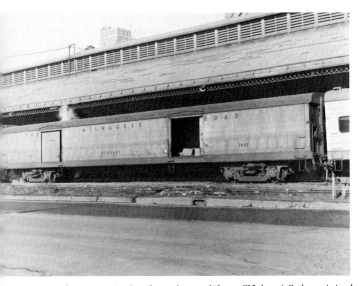

76-foot express car constructed by Milwaukee shops in 1934. The newer doors, shown here with port holes, were added later. Car 1104 was part of a series from 1100 to 1122. (Jim Scribbins)

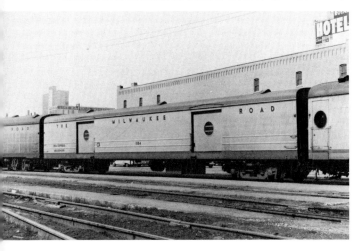

Coach 407 is a 1936 coach built by the Shops. Shown at Milwaukee on October 4, 1964. (Jim Scribbins)

Car 1955, 81 feet long, began life as "Nokomis" the original Beaver Tale parlor car in 1935. The car is shown here in Milwaukee on January 21, 1965. (Jim Scribbins)

Coach 434 was constructed in 1937 by the Milwaukee shops. Shown here at Milwaukee in July, 1964. (Jim Scribbins)

Car 183, the Elm Grove, was a Parlor-Diner built by the shops in 1948. The car was out of service after April 25, 1965. (Jim Scribbins)

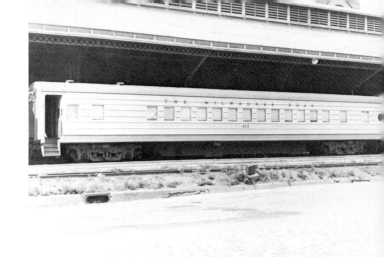

Coach 452 is representative of the cars constructed in 1938. (Jim Scribbins)

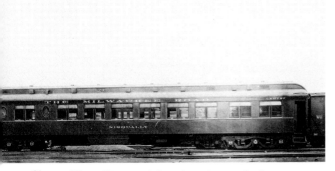

Sleeper Nisqually, containing 12 sections and 1 drawing room, was constructed in 1910 by the Pullman Company. In 1936, the car was converted to a tourist sleeper. This Milwaukee Road photo shows Nisqually in its original orange with maroon trim color scheme.

Coach 562 is a former parlor car constructed in 1938. (Jim Scribbins)

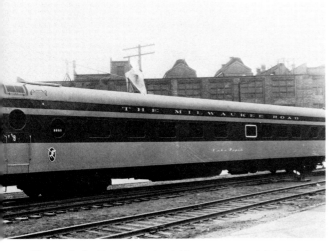

Sleeper Lake Pepin contained 10 roomettes and 6 double bedrooms. Originally built for the Olympian Hiawatha, the cars served on the Arrow after 1956. The vestibule is the rear part of the car. (Pullman-Standard)

Sleeper Lake Crescent after repainting to the new yellow and grey. (Jim Scribbins)

This photo shows the opposite side of the Lake series cars previously illustrated.

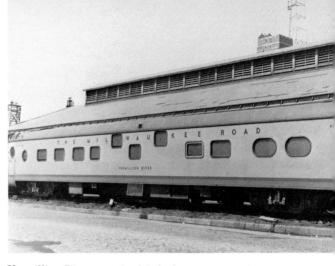

Vermillion River contained 8 duplex roomettes, 6 roomettes and 4 double bedrooms. They were operated on the Pioneer Limited and later on other trains. Built by Pullman in 1948. Car was photographed in Milwaukee by Jim Scribbins on April 25, 1964.

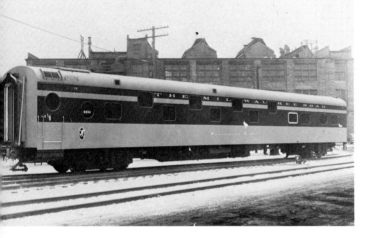

Wisconsin Dells contained 16 duplex roomettes, 4 double bedrooms with the vestibule rear of the car. The 16-4 sleepers were operated on the Pioneer Limited. (Pullman-Standard)

Raymond shows the opposite side of the 16-4 sleeper. (Jim Scribbins)

The 8-6-4 sleepers were also equipped with rear vestibules. It is interesting to note that these types of sleepers were the last to operate on the former Duluth, South Shore & Atlantic's Copper Country Limited. This train operated thru from Chicago to Calumet, Michigan over the Milwaukee Road and DSS&A, later the Soo Line. This car is making its last run, to the scrap yard at Duluth, Minnesota.

PASSENGER EQUIPMENT
REPRESENTATIVE ROSTER
1961 to 1971

Type	Car Numbers or Names	Capacity	Length Over Buffer
Super Dome Cafe Lounge	50 to 59	96	85'6"
Heater Cars	72 to 77		38'10"
Dining Lounge	104 to 108	42	82'6"
Dining Cars	109 to 112	48	82'6"
Dining Cars	115 to 126	48	85'
Dining Lounge	151	51.	82'6"
Tap	160, 161	52	82'6"
Lunch Lounge Car	164, 165	44	85'
	167	52	85'
	172, 173	44	85'
Diner Lounge	170, 171	48	85'
Cafe Parlor	180, 181	40	85'
	183, 184	40	85'
Cafe Lounge	182, 185	46	85'
Skytop Observation Parlor	186 Cedar Rapids	41	85'
	187 Coon Rapids	41	85'
	188 Dell Rapids	41	85'
	189 Priest Rapids	41	85'
Combine	206, 207	40	81'3"
Coach	400 to 435	66	82'3"
	436	72	82'3"
	437 to 452	70	82'3"
	453	72	82'3"
	454 to 478	68	82'3"
	480 to 507	66	85'
	539 to 545	66	85'
	560 to 562	62	82'3"
	563, 564	45	82'3"
	565	62	82'3"
	566	64	82'3"
	600 to 612	54	85'
	614 to 640	54	85'
	649 to 651	53	85'10"
	652 to 661	54	85'
Baggage	801, 802		64'
	826, 830		64'
	842		63'
	844, 845		63'10"
	850, 851		63'10"
	855		64'6"
	858 to 863		64'11"
	1001 to 1075		75'6"
	1076		82'11"
	1078		75'9"
	1079 to 1082		75'10"
	1095 to 1099		75'10"
	1100 to 1122		76'3"
	1123		75'9"
Rail Post Office Baggage	1200 to 1204	30' RPO	75'10"
	1205	15' RPO	75'10"
Rail Post Office Baggage	1206	30' RPO	75'10"
	1208 to 1230	30' RPO	75'
Baggage	1300 to 1307		75'10"
	1308		82'6"
Baggage Dormitory	1309 to 1316	20	75'
Baggage	1317 to 1336		75'
	1337 to 1339		81'1"
Baggage-Dorm	1350 to 1356		85'
Box-Express	1600 to 1624		54'2"
Baggage	1700 to 1721		63'10"
	1722		64'

Type	Car Numbers or Names	Capacity	Length Over Buffer
10 Rmt. 6 Bedroom Sleepers	2 Lake Couer d'Alene	22	85'
	3 Lake Keechelus	22	85'
	4 Lake Pepin	22	85'
	5 Lake Oconomowoc	22	85'
	6 Lake Pend Oreille	22	85'
	7 Lake Chatcolet	22	85'
	8 Lake Pewaukee	22	85'
	9 Lake Nashotah	22	85'
	10 Lake Kapowsin	22	85'
	11 Lake Crescent	22	85'
8 Bedroom Observ. Sky-Top Lounge	12 Alder Creek	35	85'
	14 Arrow Creek	35	85'
	15 Coffee Creek	35	85'
	16 Gold Creek	35	85'
	17 Marble Creek	35	85'
	18 Spanish Creek	35	85'
8 Duplex Rmt. 6 Rmt. 4 Bedroom Sleeper	19 Madison River	22	85'
	20 St. Joe River	22	85'
	21 Yellowstone River	22	85'
	22 Gallatin River	22	85'
	23 Vermillion River	22	85'
	24 Jefferson River	22	85'
	25 Chippewa River	22	85'
	26 Wisconsin River	22	85'
	31 Minnesota River	22	85'
	32 Zumbro River	22	85'
16 Duplex Rmt. 4 Bedroom Sleepers	27 Raymond	24	85'
	28 New Lisbon	24	85'
	29 Wisconsin Dells	24	85'
	30 Rodney	24	85'

Type	Number		Seats/RPO	Length
RPO-Baggage	1800		30' RPO	76'4"
	1824, 1825		30' RPO	63'10"
	1863 to 1867		30' RPO	75'10"
Baggage	1901 to 1913			63'
	1915 to 1923			82'11"
	1943 to 1949			82'3"
	1950 to 1960			81'9"
	1962			82'5"
	1970 to 1973			75'10"
	1974			76'4"
	1975 to 1978			75'10"
	1979			81'8"
	2000			75'9"
	2050			66'3"
Rail Post Office	2105 to 2135			65'
	2150, 2151			
	2152, 2153			
Mail and Baggage	2175		60' RPO	85'
Combines	2701 to 2707		24	59'
	2708 to 2714		24	56'
Pass, Mail & Express	2752 to 2755		24	73'7"
	2758		24	73'7"
Suburban Coaches	3300 to 3399		82 to 97	78'0" to 82'11"
	3930 to 4310 (Various numbers)			
Coaches	4400		54	82'2"
	4402 to 4440		63	82'2"
	4448		72	82'2"
Tourship Cars 14 Sections	5740	Mt. Spokane	28	85'
	5741	Mt. Washington		85'
	5742	Mt. McKinley		85'
	5743	Mt. Bosley		85'
	5744	Mt. Rainier		85'
	5745	Mt. Rushmore		85'
	5746	Mt. St. Helens		85'
	4747	Mt. Wilson		85'
	5748	Mt. Hope		85'
	5749	Mt. Stuart		85'
	5750	Mt. Harold		85'
	5751	Mt. Angeles		85'
	5752	Mt. Chittenden		85'
	5753	Mt. Jupiter		85'
	5754	Mt. Tacoma		85'

Type	Number	Name	Seats	Length
Ten Section, Two Compt. 1 Drawing Room Sleepers		Arrowhead	27	83'
		Hartland		
		Iron Mountain		
		Puget Sound		
		Tomah		
		Tomahawk		
		Big Rock		
		Des Moines		
		Pewaukee		
		Watertown		
		Wauwatosa		
8 Section, 2 Compt. 1 Drawing Room Sleepers		Michigamme	23	83'
		Okoboji		
		Ontonagon		
		Pahasahpa		
Beaver Tail Parlor Cars		Miller	45	82'
		Mitchell		
Parlor Cars	190	Maple Valley	35	85'
	191	Wisconsin Valley		
	192	Gallatin Valley		
	193	Fox River Valley		
	194	Red River Valley		
	195	Pleasant Valley		
	196	Rock Valley		
	197	Spring Valley		
Motor Cars	5900 to 5901			85'
10 Rmt. 6 Bedroom Sleepers	33	Pacific Bridge	22	85'
	34	Pacific Cruiser		
	35	Pacific Guard		
	36	Pacific Harbor		
	37	Pacific Light		
Bi-Level Coaches	300 to 341		162	85'
	380 to 399		156	85'
Passenger Flexi-Van Cars	58018 to 58038			80'9"
Business Cars		Montana		
		Milwaukee		
		Wisconsin		
		Indiana		

Chapter 3
The Hiawathas

The Milwaukee Road's Hiawatha streamliners, it can be said, were among the finest and most popular trains in North America. That is a bold statement to be sure, but let's look at some of the reasons why this is so.

First of all, only the Southern Pacific's Coast Daylight exceeded the Twin Cities Afternoon Hiawatha in revenue earned. This says a lot for the Milwaukee Road because the Hiawathas competed with some superb streamliners, the 400's and the Zephyrs, whereas the Southern Pacific did not have any competition that could match the comfort of the Daylight. It is difficult to know what the Hiawatha would have done in the Chicago-Minneapolis market without the Burlington and Chicago & North Western. However, it is probably safe to say that it would have outdone the Daylight.

Another factor is that during the days of decline, it was the Hiawathas which lasted the longest. On Amtrak day, there was no 400 and only a Zephyr stub—a three car Morning Zephyr between Chicago and the Twin Cities. On the other hand, the Milwaukee Road's Morning Hiawatha was still a full-sized train complete with luxury coaches, buffeteria dining car, Super Dome with cafe lounge and last, but not least, a drawing room parlor car. True, the Skytop Parlor was gone but parlor car services were still provided in the true Hiawatha tradition dating back to May 29, 1935.

Hiawatha service was provided on all of the important routes of the Milwaukee Road's Lines East. In the early 1950's, one could ride Hiawathas between the following points:

All together there was a maximum fleet of six Hiawathas, all of which operated over the Lines East with the Olympian Hi the only train to carry sleepers and also operate on both Lines East and West.

All trains offered parlor car service, usually in the form of a Beaver-tail or Skytop. Dining service was provided by either full diners or the fantastic Tip-Top-Tap cars. With the exception of the Olympian Hi, all were powered before dieselization by streamlined steam in the form of Atlantics, Pacifics, Hudsons and even Ten-wheelers. No other road had such a variety of streamlined steam, and there were a number of engines painted in Hiawatha schemes for substitute service.

Super Domes were added to three Hiawathas in 1952. Both Twin Cities trains and the Olympian became domeliners, and the traveling public had a choice of three Super Domeliner Hiawathas in each direction between Chicago and the Twin Cities. What more could the traveler desire?

Slowly but surely, much of the Hiawatha fleet fell victim to the automobile. The Mid-West Hiawatha was discontinued in April, 1956, after having been combined with the Union Pacific's Challenger between Chicago and Omaha. With both day and night service offered by the Chicago & North Western, Burlington and the Rock Island between Chicago and Omaha, the Milwaukee Road did not see the need to continue operating the Mid-West Hi on a day schedule — especially since there were four streamliners in each direction on the route that offered morning service to Chicago and evening service to Omaha.

Chicago-St. Paul-Minneapolis	Trains 5 and 6	Morning Hiawatha
	Trains 100 and 102	Afternoon Hiawatha
Chicago-Seattle	Trains 15 and 16	Olympian Hiawatha
Chicago-Woodruff, Wisc.	Trains 200 and 201 (Operated in connection with 100 & 101 at New Lisbon)	North Woods Hiawatha
Chicago-Omaha-Sioux Falls	Trains 102-132 and 103-133	Midwest Hiawatha
Chicago-Ontonagon, Mich.	Trains 14 and 21	Chippewa Hiawatha

By 1960, the Milwaukee Road had discontinued most of the secondary fleet and had already combined the Olympian and Afternoon Hiawatha westbound between Chicago and Minneapolis, and the Olympian and Morning Hi eastbound earlier in 1957. The traveler still had a choice of two Super Dome Hiawathas each way daily. Except for the discontinuance of the Olympian Hi altogether in 1966, there would be virtually no change in Hiawatha service for ten years between Chicago and the Twin Cities. The Milwaukee Road became known as the one road you could count on to travel between Chicago, Milwaukee and Minnesota complete with a bus connection to and from Duluth-Superior. One by one the competitors gave up their services, but the Milwaukee Road remained without downgrading the Hiawathas in any way.

Excessive expenses forced the discontinuance of the Afternoon Hiawatha in January, 1970, but the Morning Hi rolled on until Amtrak day.

Admittedly, this is an extremely brief historical sketch of the Milwaukee Road Hiawathas. Should the reader desire a complete history of the Hiawathas, he or she should read the excellent book

THE HIAWATHA STORY
By Jim Scribbins
Kalmbach Publishing Company
Milwaukee, Wisconsin
Copyright 1970

The name Hiawatha lived on through 1978 on Milwaukee Road trackage with the so-called "Hiawatha Service" between Chicago and Milwaukee, and also the "Twin Cities Hiawatha" between Chicago and Minneapolis. Although the former consisted of Milwaukee Road coaches, they bore little resemblance to the grand Hiawathas of yesteryear. Indeed, in May, 1976, Turbos replaced the Hiawatha Service Trains. It is still the hope of many people, rail-fans and shall we say, non-rail fan train travelers, that the Hiawathas will some day return. Although it is doubtful, one never knows what the future will bring. However, there is one thing that we can be sure of without reservation, the *Hiawathas* rank high among the finest streamliner fleets in the world.

Before going into service in 1935, the new Hiawathas were admired by thousands. The new train is on exhibit at the Chicago Union Station in this photo. (The Milwaukee Road)

Train 101 rounds the curve and crosses Canal Street north of the Union Station on its fast run from Chicago to Minneapolis. (The Milwaukee Road)

The "Hiawatha" did more for the Milwaukee Road's fame than any other single service the "Road" offered. Superbly designed, super powered by a streamlined Atlantic, the train outdid either the Zephyr or the 400 of 1935. The "Hi" was truly a masterpiece of passenger train design. This photo was taken at Tower A-20, otherwise known as the Techney Cut-off north of Chicago. (The Milwaukee Road)

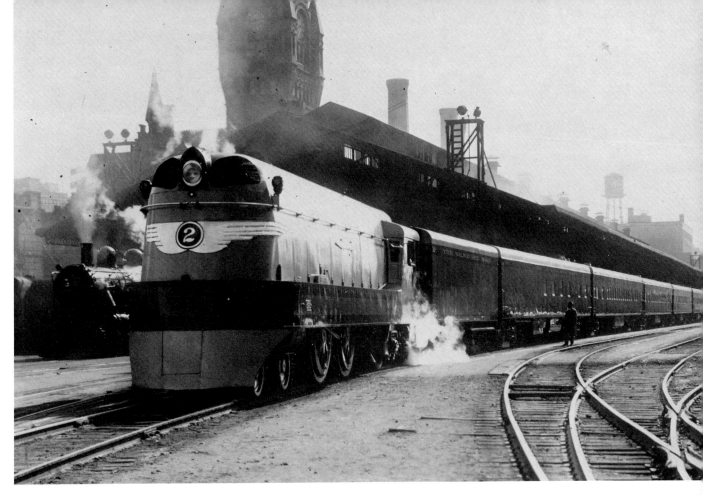

The original "Hiawatha" went on display at several locations before going into service. This photo shows the train on exhibit at Milwaukee. The reader may be interested to know that a man by the name of Hiawatha did indeed exist. He was a peacemaker and was responsible for bringing together the Mohawks, Oneidas, Senecas, Cayugas and Onondaga, and forming the Iroquois nation. Hiawatha, himself, was a Mohawk. In view of the task Hiawatha accomplished, it was indeed appropriate that the Milwaukee Road name a fleet of streamliners after the man; although it is doubtful that any of the originators of the name realized the significance of Hiawatha's great deed. It was Longfellow's poetry that produced the name for the streamliner fleet. (The Milwaukee Road)

President Scandrett (half way up the stairs), who was responsible for much of the Hiawatha idea, looks on as Jeannie Dixon, daughter of the General Passenger Agent, prepares to christen train 101 prior to its departure from Chicago for the first time. (The Milwaukee Road)

The Milwaukee Atlantics were superb high speed machines, indeed outdoing the Metroliners of Penn Central produced more than three decades later. Driving off the front driver, the 4-4-2's were similar to Canadian Pacific's 4-4-4 Jubilee engines. (George-Paterson Collection and Milwaukee Road)

Pacific 6160 was a rarity. Converted to oil and painted Hiawatha colors for protection power on the Hiawatha. Photo taken at Chicago on October 15, 1935. (George-Paterson Collection)

The Hiawatha is being readied for the trip from the Western Avenue coach yards to the Union Station. The eight-car train was perfectly matched inside and out. It is 1936 and the Hiawatha's career was just beginning, a career that would make railroad history. (Harold K. Vollrath Collection)

The pride that the Milwaukee Road had in its Hiawatha was reflected in the use of a color painting of the train crossing the bridge at Wisconsin Dells. The painting was used on the 1938 art calendar. (The Milwaukee Road)

The 4400 series coaches used on the early Hiawatha were among the finest operated on any railroad in 1934 and 1935. Note the deep cushions for a high travel comfort index — such was travel on the Hiawatha. (The Milwaukee Road)

The 1935 Hiawatha parlor cars were even more comfortable than the coaches. However, the Beaver-tail parlor had seats facing forward in the observation end. Note the wood paneling. (The Milwaukee Road)

Right — The interior of the Beaver tail parlor car carried in the new 1937 Hiawatha. (The Milwaukee Road)

The 1935 "Hi" steams along the Chicago & Milwaukee Division with the first Beaver-tail bringing up the markers end. In many ways, the beaver-tail reminds one of the tail end of a Ford built during the 1930's. (The Milwaukee Road)

The popularity of the train led to two-section running. This photo shows two sections lined up at the Union Station in Chicago on January 16th, 1936. (The Milwaukee Road)

With the popularity of the "Hi", the Road re-equipped the train in late 1936 and early 1937. This photo shows the two ribbed side car, the Omeme, a parlor observation Beaver-tail. The windows in the second train were squared off as opposed to the curved tops of the original train. The car is shown at Milwaukee on September 29, 1936. (The Milwaukee Road)

The new 1937 train was also painted orange and maroon. This photo of the 401 clearly shows the wide diaphragm arrangement and how it was painted to reflect not only the paint scheme, but also the double ribs above and below the windows. (The Milwaukee Road)

This photo shows the interior of the new 1937 train dining car. Note the "Hiawatha" menus on the outside of the tables. Again, the Milwaukee made extensive use of wood for the interiors, giving the cars a very cozy effect. (The Milwaukee Road)

Heavy traffic necessitated heavier steam power and so new streamlined Hudsons went into service in 1939. This publicity photo was taken to dramatize the Hiawathas, two a day each way between Chicago, Milwaukee, St. Paul and Minneapolis. (The Milwaukee Road)

The third set of equipment makes a test trip with the white flags flying indicating a passenger extra. It is the late summer of 1939 and the train is rounding a curve west of downtown Milwaukee on the old LaCrosse Division. (The Milwaukee Road)

The third set of equipment had an additional maroon band through the window area with a grey roof. This is coach 445. (The Milwaukee Road)

The third set of equipment provided seating looking out of the Beaver tail, a splendid innovation. (The Milwaukee Road)

The interior of the dining cars used on the third set of Hiawatha equipment, and also the first Morning Hiawatha of 1939. (The Milwaukee Road)

The 1939 train also used wood paneling and trim extensively, and the coach windows were in groups of three. The seating was as comfortable or more so then the previous two sets of Hiawatha equipment. (The Milwaukee Road)

Interior of the parlor observation Beaver-tail. Note the use of carpeting with an Indian design. The windows were also in groups of three with draperies covering the edge of the windows, every third post. Soft, reclining, rotating seats provided the maximum daytime comfort index for the Chicago - Minneapolis run. (The Milwaukee Road)

A pair of interesting tap cars were built in 1942 for the Afternoon Hiawatha. Cars 160 and 161 operated on 100 and 101 until 1948, when they were shifted to the Morning Hi, trains 5 and 6. (The Milwaukee Road)

The cars contained 12 tap seats and 40 lounge seats in an unusual arrangement. Instead of passengers moving thru the center of the car, the passageway was along one side which permitted people to enjoy their leisure without the interruption of passengers moving through. The Milwaukee constructed only two cars with this design. Note the extensive use of wood and the Indian motif. (The Milwaukee Road)

The ultimate in Hiawatha design came in 1948 with the last new equipment going into service. Here we see the Hiawatha crossing the Mississippi River after departing Minneapolis for Chicago. (The Milwaukee Road)

The 1948 train carried the Sky-top Parlor cars, which represented the ultimate in parlor observation car design. The eastbound train 100 is shown here along the Mississippi River at St. Paul. (The Milwaukee Road)

An example of 1948 coach (No. 554) after being repainted in the yellow and grey with red lettering. (The Milwaukee Road)

The parlor car "Red River Valley" was built for Hiawatha service in 1948. She contained 30 reclining rotating seats, drawing room and men's washroom at the vestibule or forward end, and the ladies' washroom at the rear end. The car is shown on train 5, the Morning Hi, at the old depot in Milwaukee in July, 1965. (Jim Scribbins)

Tap cars included wood for the decor and flowing lines with circular tables and sofas. The 1948 cars were used on the Hi's until the Super Domes arrived in 1952. At that time they were assigned to other trains. For example, when this photo was taken in early 1964, this car was in service on train 9 between Chicago and Milwaukee on the Copper Country Limited. (Jim Scribbins)

Dining on the 1948 Hiawathas was a superb experience. The motif included indirect lighting and again a liberal use of wood was part of the decor. (The Milwaukee Road)

The 1948 Afternoon Hiawatha, train 101, highballs along the Mississippi River between LaCrosse and Winona. (The Milwaukee Road)

1952 brought the Super Domes, which replaced the tap cars and converted the Morning, Afternoon and Olympian Hiawathas into "Super Domeliners." This photo shows train 100 running the wrong main between Winona and LaCrosse on the old LaCrosse Division. (The Milwaukee Road)

Train 100 passes through the Lower Dells of the Wisconsin River at Wisconsin Dells. (The Milwaukee Road)

67

The new Super Domes were the first cars not to have the maroon letter board. They introduced the final orange and maroon paint style. (The Milwaukee Road)

Interior views of the dome, which was the first to extend to full length of the car. (The Milwaukee Road)

For a short period of time the cafe section of the Super Dome served light meals. Later the below dome area was used only for beverage service with all food being served in the diner. They did provide a limited menu on the Minneapolis-Deer Lodge trains 15 and 16, after the Olympian Hi had been discontinued. (The Milwaukee Road)

The Morning Hi, train 5, arrives at Wisconsin Dells behind a streamlined Hudson in the year 1946. (Russ Porter)

It is 1968 and train 5 barrels through the Wisconsin Dells area with a long train, still requiring 3 diesel units. (Russ Porter)

Train 101, the Afternoon Hi, departs Milwaukee for Minneapolis in early 1947 and is breaking in the new power for the forthcoming Olympian Hiawatha. (Russ Porter)

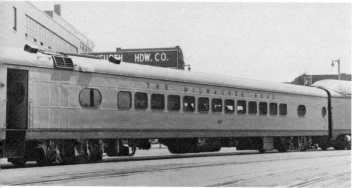

Train 5 handled a substantial amount of head-end traffic. This photo shows the Morning Hi leaving Milwaukee in November, 1962 with one E-9 and two FP-7's for power. Note the 50 foot Milwaukee Road express box car ahead of the Great Northern baggage car in the train. (Jim Scribbins)

A number of the 1948 coaches were rebuilt with leg rest seats and renumbered in the 600 series. One interesting innovation with the 1948 cars was in the non-vestibule end of the car. When passing from one car to another, one could simply step into the coach and then open the door to enter. This was different from other cars where the door was immediately adjacent to the diaphragm. (Jim Scribbins)

Super Dome in the yellow and grey color scheme. (Jim Scribbins)

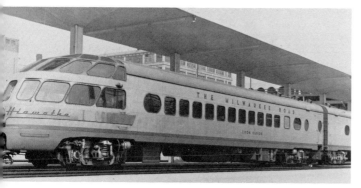

Sky-top Parlor car "Coon Rapids" on train 6 at Milwaukee in September, 1965. This equipment stood more for the individuality of the Milwaukee Road than any other equipment. (Jim Scribbins)

What was once the fine North Woods Hiawatha, an Alco RSC-2 handles a 1934 express car and two 1942 coaches on train 203 just north of the Necedah depot on July 25, 1959. (Jim Scribbins)

Westbound train 103, the Midwest Hiawatha is powered by a type A Atlantic at Savanna, Illinois in December, 1940. (W. S. Kuba Collection)

Diesels arrived later, and here we see 103 again with two EMD
units near Elgin, Illinois. (Russ Porter)

Train 103 just east of Elgin, Illinois in 1946. (Russ Porter)

Train 102, the Midwest Hi, slides into Council Bluffs, Iowa with
an E unit and four cars in June, 1947. The baggage man will
load some express, and a lone soldier hoists his duffel bag over
his shoulder to prepare to board the "Hi." (Harold K. Vollrath
Collection)

Train 14, the Chippewa Hiawatha, passes through Pembine, Wisconsin in August, 1947 with 7 cars at 40 miles per hour. (George-Paterson Collection)

The combined North Woods Hi and Chippewa Hi slams through Roundout on July 31, 1947 with 14 cars at 95 miles per hour. The front portion of the train to the baggage car is the North Woods portion, while the Chip makes up the last seven cars. (George-Paterson Collection)

Train 21, the Chippewa Hi rolls through Roundout, Illinois with 6 cars at 90 miles per hour. (George-Paterson Collection)

The Olympian Hiawatha, train 15, bangs through Roundout over the EJ&E crossing at 100 miles per hour with 11 cars. Few trains could compare with the beauty and luxury of the Olympian Hi. (Harold K. Vollrath Collection)

The Olympian Hi, train 16, passes Lake Pewaukee, Wisconsin
with Fairbanks-Morse power doing the honors on the head-end.
(The Milwaukee Road)

This mail and baggage car, No. 1210, was originally built for the Olympian Hi. Note the unusual color arrangement of the maroon window band. Later the car was re-assigned to the Southwest Limited, the Chippewa and other trains. (The Milwaukee Road)

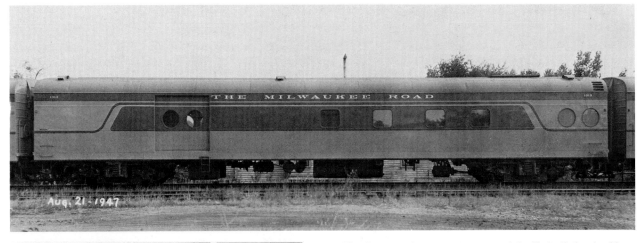

This baggage-dormitory car was originally built for the Olympian Hi, but also served on the Pioneer Limited. Later a number of Touralux cars were converted to baggage-dorms for the "City" trains and the conversions were easily recognizable by their vestibules. (The Milwaukee Road)

One of the finest innovations by the Milwaukee was the Touralux cars. Open section economy sleepers, the cars were the only such equipment built. They were constructed during a time when all roads were phasing out such service, with the exception of the Soo Line Railroad. (The Milwaukee Road)

Pullman Standard built the Sky-top Lounge sleepers for the Olympian Hi. The cars contained 8 double bedrooms and put the finishing touches to a fine train. (The Milwaukee Road)

Beaver tails and Sky-tops
A Milwaukee Road Trade Mark

(All photos Milwaukee Road)

The insignia of Hiawatha will long be remembered in the hearts of many rail travelers. It stood for speed, safety, comfort and dependable rail travel, and it is sadly missed by many, many people.

Chapter 4
Suburban Trains

Over the years, the Milwaukee Road operated commuter trains on three lines in two districts. The most widely known is the Chicago Suburban Territory between Chicago and Elgin, Illinois, and Chicago-Walworth, Wisconsin. Known as the West Line and the North Line, the routes are 37 miles and 74 miles long respectively. There has been a suburban service on these routes ever since the original construction days. The future of the Fox Lake-Walworth section is, as of this writing, questionable. The Milwaukee would like to discontinue that segment.

The second route was the Milwaukee-Watertown line, 46 miles, which served the suburbs west of Milwaukee.

The Chicago Suburban Territory has had its ups and downs during the last 75 years. For most of that time, up until the 1950's, the two lines were operated with steam and hand-me-down coaches. Some of the equipment was even downgraded sleeping cars with the air conditioning bubbles left in place. The original seating was replaced with brown walk-over seats. The cars were painted in Hiawatha color schemes, orange and maroon with black roof. The paint schemes varied with each change in the Hi color arrangements, and frequently commuter trains could be made up with two or three schemes.

The train service was always lighter in frequency than any of the other heavy suburban services. In the Chicago area, there were 6 railroads offering frequent suburban service: Illinois Central, Burlington, South Shore, Rock Island, Chicago & North Western and the Milwaukee Road. The Milwaukee Road did not experience any substantial growth or change in its services until the 1950's when the territory served by the railroad came under residential development. At the same time the road began replacing steam with diesel locomotives on the suburban runs.

Diesel power in the form of Electro-Motive geeps and Fairbanks-Morse road-switchers dominated the scene, and they did not look bad coupled to a string of orange and maroon coaches. The actual service remained much the same. By the late 1950's, Electro-Motive E-7's and "F" units were being operated in suburban service, but still the changes in train service were very few. It was a static service for the public, and a drain on the Milwaukee's pocketbook. Changes had to be made and would soon be forthcoming in the form of new passenger equipment, bi-level stainless steel commuter cars that depended upon diesel generators for lighting, heating and air-conditioning. That in itself does not sound unusual, but in this case the generators were located in the locomotive. The Milwaukee Road was switching from steam to electric power (from the locomotive) to maintain all of the comfort services on board the train. This change, introduced in 1961, was the first major change for the Milwaukee Road since dieselization. With this change, yellow "E" and "F" units replaced nearly all of the road-switchers.

By the mid-1960's, the Milwaukee Road completely replaced all standard or heavy-weight equipment with the stainless steel bi-level cars. Furthermore, the trains were now push-pull with cab cars located at the end of each train. Following C&NW operating practice, the push-pull trains push to Chicago and pull to the suburbs. A very modern operation to say the least, and with a few exceptions, the Milwaukee Road has experienced increases in ridership in every year since 1960.

Despite these increases in ridership, the Milwaukee Road still suffered from commutation losses as a result of the operation. In 1971, the Northwest Suburban Mass Transit and the North Suburban Mass Transit Districts were formed. These districts were eligible to receive Federal Funding under the Urban Mass Transportation Act of 1964. The West Line and North Line were turned over to these two districts respectively in the early 1970's, and the result has been the purchase of additional bi-level stainless steel equipment and 15 Electro-Motive F40C's.

The new F40C's are something else again. They are among the newest passenger motive power developed in the United States. Thirteen are

Non-rush hour train 228 races through Bensenville on the West Line en route to Chicago with 2 cars in early October, 1949. (George-Paterson Collection)

owned by the NESMT, while two are owned by the NSMTD. The units look right at home at the head-end of the bi-level cars, which have a roof line only slightly higher than the new style "F" units. All equipment, both coaches and motive power, was turned over to the two transit districts, which in turn has leased the equipment back to the Milwaukee for operation.

To give one an idea of the change in service, this writer reported that the Milwaukee Road carried approximately 22,000 passengers on 64 week-day runs in 1969. (*Commuter Railroads,* Superior Publishing Company, 1970, p. 117) In early 1976, the Milwaukee is operating 81 week-day trains and carrying approximately 30,000 passengers every week-day. Also in 1976, the Milwaukee became the first Chicago railroad to sign an agreement with the regional transportation authority.

The service is greatly appreciated by the suburbanites, and it provides what this writer has expounded on so much before, the only all-weather transportation to and from those communities. This is the most exciting era for Milwaukee Road suburban service, and the future looks very bright.

The Milwaukee's second most important suburban service was the Milwaukee-Watertown run. It was discontinued on July 31, 1972, the victim of excessive costs, the automobile and the failure of government leaders to see the wisdom of rail services.

The Milwaukee Road's Cannon Ball, as trains 23 and 12 were called, had a very unusual history. Originally, No. 23 was a through Chicago-Madison train via Milwaukee. No. 23 departed Chicago at about 3:35 P.M. and arrived in Milwaukee at 5:00 P.M. Fifteen minutes later she departed making all stops to Watertown, and then continuing on to Madison. For part of her Chicago-Madison service she was equipped with a parlor and dining buffet service as well as reclining seat coaches.

Eastbound No. 12 originated at Watertown at 6:45 A.M. and made all stops to Milwaukee arriving there at 8:05 A.M. At 9:45 A.M., No. 12 continued on to Chicago after the arrival of No. 28 from Madison. No. 28 was the opposite side of 23's service to Madison in the evening.

This arrangement continued through the 1950's. However, by 1960, 23 no longer continued to Madison after making all stops to Watertown. No. 23 terminated at Watertown with a new schedule leaving Milwaukee at 5:20 P.M. and arriving at its final terminal at 6:30 P.M. Eastbound 12 departed at 6:35 A.M. with a 7:40 A.M. arrival in Milwaukee. Thus the train had become a true commuter run.

There were to be no more or few changes in 23 and 12's schedule. Indeed, in 1970, 23 departed Milwaukee at 5:25 P.M. (only five minutes difference from 10 years previous) with a 6:35 P.M. arrival. Eastbound 12 was identical.

During its operation as a pure commutation train, she was powered by a single diesel unit, either a road-switcher or an E or F unit. Normal consist was but 2 coaches, generally Hiawatha cars of a by-gone era.

No. 23 did carry a third coach on its final trip. She was a neat little train and served her passengers well. There just weren't enough of them.

And this ends the chapter on Milwaukee Road suburban services, which fortunately continues to grow in the Chicago Area. The Milwaukee Road has done a fine job of transporting people to and from Chicago, and the company is to be commended for its efforts to maintain and expand a needed service.

Looking more like a local than a suburban train, 144 is powered by Pacific No. 190 as it moves toward the Windy City south of Roundout. The power and cars are typical of the early post war period. This photo was taken July 31, 1947. (George-Paterson Collection)

CHICAGO MILWAUKEE ST. PAUL AND PACIFIC

Daylight Saving Time — One Hour Faster than Central Time

To CHICAGO

READ DOWN — **WEEK-DAY TRAINS** — READ DOWN

SOUTHBOU[ND] — Where time is [...] trains do not [...]

Column 22 = **THE SIOUX** From Mitchell, Sioux Falls, Mason City
Column 156 = **THE VARSITY**

30	132	32	36	136	48	42	138	22	140	144	142	44	156	146	Southbound
							AM	AM			AM			PM	
							6.50	7.36			11.22			7.44	Lv. .... Walworth
							7.00				f11.30			d 7.53	.... Zenda
							f 7.08							a 8.02	.... Hebron To
							f 7.16							a 8.10	.... Solon Mills
							f 7.19							8.13	.... Spring Gro
	AM			AM										PM	
	5.52			6.40			7.27		8.15	11.20	11.56		7.49	b	.... Fox Lake
	5.55			6.44			7.30		8.18	11.23	c		7.53	b	.... Ingleside
	a 5.56			a 6.45			a 7.31		a 8.19	a 11.24	c		a 7.54	b	.... Wilson Roa
	6.00			6.49			7.34		8.22	11.27	c		7.57	b	.... Long Lake
	6.04			6.53			7.38		8.25	11.31	c		8.01	b	.... Round La
	6.09			6.58			7.43		8.30	11.36	c		8.05	b	.... Grays Lak
	6.17			7.07			7.51		8.39	11.44	c		8.16	b	.... Libertyvil
	6.24						7.57		8.45	11.50			f 8.23	b	.... Rondout
	6.29			f 7.18			8.02		8.50	f11.55			f 8.28	e	.... West Lake F
AM		AM			AM	AM					PM	PM			
6.00	6.35	6 55		7.24	7.32	7.50	8.07		8.55	12.00		6.25	8.33	e	.... Deerfield
6.04	6.39	7.00		7.29	7.36	7.55			9.01	12.03		6.30	8.38	e	.... Northbroo
f 6.06	6.41				f 7.39	7.57			f 9.03	12.06		6.32	8.40	e	.... Techny
6.10	6.45	7 06		7.35	7.44	8.02			9.08	12.10		6.37	8.45	e	.... Glenview
f 6.12	f 6.48	7 09		7.41	7.49	f 8.05			f 9.11	12.12		6.40	8.48	e	.... Golf
6.15	6.52	7 12		7.49		8.08			9.14	12.15		6.42	8.51	e	.... Morton Gr
			AM												
6.19	6.56	7 17	7.33		7.54	8.12			9.18	12.19		6.47	8.55	e	.... Edgebrook (Devo
6.21	7.00	7.20	7.38		7.57	8.15			9.21	12.21		6.50	8.58	e	.... Forest Glen (Elst
6.23	7.03	7.23	7.41		8.01				9.23	12.23		6.52	9.00	e	.... Mayfair (Montro
6.25	7.05	7.25	7.44		8.04				9.27	12.25		6.55	9.03		.... Grayland (Milwau
6.29	7.09	7.29	7.48	7.52	8.08	8.22			9.30	12.30		6.58	9.06		.... Healy (Fullerto
6.35	7.15	7.35	7.54	7.58	8.14	8.28	8.31	9.18	9.35	12.37	12.52	7.04	9.12	9.18	.... Western Ave. (ne
6.45	7.25	7.45	8.04	8.08	8.23	8.38	8.41	9.30	9.45	12.47	1.05	7.15	9.23	9.30	Ar. .... Union Stat
															Canal., Adams St. &
AM	AM	AM	AM	AM	AM	AM	AM	AM	AM	PM	PM	PM	PM	PM	

REFERENCE MARKS

⊕No agent at this Station.
a—Stops on signal to take passengers for Chicago and estern Ave.
b—Stops to leave passengers from Bardwell and beyond.
c—Stops to leave passengers from Janesville or beyond.
d—Stops to take passengers for Chicago; also to leave passengers from beyond Walworth.
e—Stops to leave passengers from Walworth and beyond.
f—Stops on signal to take or leave passengers.

EQUIPMENT

Club Car—Radio on Train 22.
Parlor Solarium Car on Train 146.
Parlor Car on Train 142.
Parlor Car Service on Train 22.
Dining Car Service on Trains 22 and 146.   Coaches on All Trains.

HOLIDAY TRAIN SERVICE

On New Year's Day, Memorial Day, July 4th, Labor Day, Thanksgiving and Christmas, all strictly suburban trains will be run on Sunday schedules.

LOST AND FOUND

Don't forget your parcels. Any loss should be reported immediately to General Baggage Department, 221 Union Station Bldg., Chicago, or inquiry made at South Side Baggage Checking Counter, Union Station—*will not be responsible* for unchecked articles left in stations or cars.

The PIONEER LIM[ITED]

The Pioneer Limited with its luxuriou[s] [...] been the favorite for night travel, and i[s] [...]

Northbound

Union Station   Da[ily]
Lv. Chicago.............10:15
Lv. Milwaukee..........11:55
Ar. St. Paul............7:30
Ar. Minneapolis........8:00
Milwaukee Station

Bedroom Lounge Car—Pull[man]
Dining Car

Passenger equipment assigned to the commuters, before the bi-levels, came directly from the classic era. Coach 3394 was an ex-14 section Pullman sleeper. The photo was taken at Elgin on August 29, 1964. (Jim Scribbins)

Daylight Saving Time
ne Hour Faster than Central Time

(Chicago Milwaukee St. Paul and Pacific logo)

READ DOWN	**SUNDAY TRAINS**				
134	22	148	154	156	146
.....	AM 7.36	AM 10.45	.....	.....	PM 7.44
.....		10.55	.....	.....	d 7 53
.....		f11.02	.....	.....	a 8 02
AM		f11.06	PM	PM	a 8 10
		11.10			8.13
7.15	.....	11.20	4.30	7 49	b
7.18		11.23	4.33	7 53	b
a 7.19		a11.24	a 4.34	a 7 54	.....
7 21		11.27	4.37	7 57	b
7.25		11.31	4.41	8 01	b
7.30		11.36	4.46	8.05	b
7.38		11.44	4.52	8 16	b
7.45		11.50	4 59	f 8 23	b
7.50		f11.55	f 5.04	f 8 28	e
7.55		12 01	5.10	8 33	e
8.00		12 04	5.14	8 38	e
f 8 02		12 06	5.16	8 40	e
8 07		12 10	5.20	8 45	e
f 8.10		12 12	5 24	8 48	e
8.13		12 15	5 27	8.51	e
8.17		12 19	5.32	8 55	e
8.20		12.21	5 34	8 58	e
8 22		12 24	5.36	9 00	e
8 24		12 27	5.39	9 03	.....
8 27		12 30	5.42	9 06	.....
8 33	9 .18	12.40	5.49	9 12	9 18
8.43	9.30	12.50	6.00	9 23	9 30
AM	AM	PM	PM	PM	PM

(Vertical labels: THE SIOUX — From Mitchell, Sioux Falls, Mason City; THE VARSITY)

between Chicago—Milwaukee—St. Paul—Minneapolis

...ioned equipment of the latest type has long ...ating on a faster, more convenient schedule.

Southbound

Milwaukee Station	Daily
Lv. Minneapolis	11:15 p.m.
Lv. St. Paul	11:49 p.m.
Ar. Milwaukee	6:00 a.m.
Ar. Chicago	7:50 a.m.

Union Station

...dard Sleeping Cars—Club Car— ...Luxury Coaches

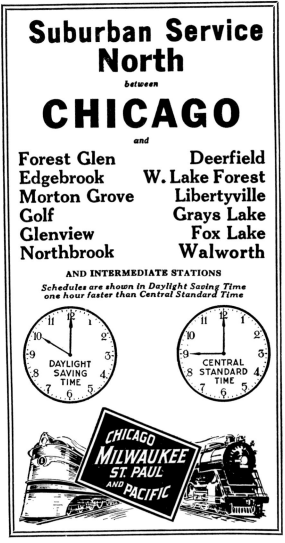

Suburban Service North
between
CHICAGO
and

Forest Glen	Deerfield
Edgebrook	W. Lake Forest
Morton Grove	Libertyville
Golf	Grays Lake
Glenview	Fox Lake
Northbrook	Walworth

AND INTERMEDIATE STATIONS
Schedules are shown in Daylight Saving Time one hour faster than Central Standard Time

DAYLIGHT SAVING TIME   CENTRAL STANDARD TIME

Coach 3350 was a typical standard suburban car with 92 seats. The car was still in service in 1964. (Jim Scribbins)

Another local looking commuter, train 211 departs the Bensenville depot with a baggage, combine and coach in October, 1949. Baggage cars provided express service on some Milwaukee Road trains plus carried newspapers to the suburbs from Chicago. (George-Paterson Collection)

A heavier train, with heavier power, Hudson 137 leads a westbound train over the Chicago & North Western diamonds at Mayfair, Illinois in October, 1952. (George-Paterson Collection)

It is evident that dieselization has taken its toll on the main lines as Hudson 128 leads an eastbound commuter from Fox Lake, Illinois. The train is a "Holiday" schedule to Chicago for it is July 4, 1953. (George-Paterson Collection)

Pacifics, such as the 888, were standard power on many Milwaukee Road passenger trains, including commuter runs out of Chicago. This one is between suburban runs at Elgin, Illinois in June, 1948. (Harold K. Vollrath Collection)

Ten-wheelers, too, ran to the suburbs, such as the 1133, shown here at the intermediate terminal of Deerfield on the North Line. The date is August 7, 1935. (George-Paterson Collection)

Car 3396 was another former Pullman sleeper downgraded for suburban service. Milwaukee Road suburban "standard era" equipment was the last to carry the classic orange and maroon, and none of the cars were ever painted yellow and grey with red trim and lettering. (Jim Scribbins)

Bi-level stainless steel coaches replaced the classic era cars, and have played a part in attracting additional commuters to ride the train. Highly comfortable, the cars are now in service on all Milwaukee Road trains such as this mid-day run to Elgin. The photo was taken on an extremely hot (98 degrees) cloudy, smoggy day in Chicago during early August, 1971. (Patrick C. Dorin)

Walworth, Wisconsin was, for many years, the final terminal for the North Line commuter service although most trains terminated at Fox Lake. One pair rush hour trains per day served the community with no service on Saturday or Sunday. Walworth is but 65 miles from Madison, the Badger State capitol that has been clamoring for re-newed passenger service to Chicago ever since Amtrak day. (Russ Porter)

Service in the mid-1970's finds additional trains, more bi-level coaches than ever and new motive power on both commuter routes. Here we see train 2231 (Oh yes, new, more complicated numbers with four digits now designate Milwaukee commuter trains.) arriving at Roselle, Illinois at 6:26 p.m. on August 3, 1976. (Patrick C. Dorin)

Train 2229 is a Chicago-Bartlet rush hour run. From that point it proceeds empty to Spaulding to cross over and return to Chicago as an equipment train. Engine No. 51 is also named the Village of Ontarioville. (Patrick C. Dorin)

Train 2227 operates as a Chicago-Elgin express train during the evening rush hour. The new motive power carries both the Milwaukee Road insignia and the Northwest Suburban Mass Transit District. Motive power on the North line carries lettering for the North Suburban Mass Transit District. Colors are predominently blue and white, with safety stripes across the nose. (Patrick C. Dorin)

All Milwaukee Road suburban equipment are bi-level stainless steel coaches. Part of the fleet is equipped with cabs at one end for the push-pull operation now quite common in the Chicago area. (Patrick C. Dorin)

The push-pull concept is demonstrated here as a westbound rush hour train departs Roselle, and an equipment train picks up speed after having waited in the clear for the westbound to unload passengers. The train on the left is headed toward Chicago on the double track main line, which is signaled for operation in both directions. (Patrick C. Dorin)

Once quite common, FP-7 and E-8 and 9's are no longer the backbone of the suburban fleet. This FP-7 is backing to the Union Station in Chicago to take out a single car train for Fox Lake on the North line. (Patrick C. Dorin)

An eastbound equipment train passes Roselle at speed after running west as train 2221 to Bartlett, and then proceeding to Spaulding, crossing over to the eastbound main and returning to Chicago.

Chapter 5

The Milwaukee Road and Amtrak

Since May 1, 1971, passenger train service on the Milwaukee Road has been operated by the National Railroad Passenger Corporation, known as Amtrak. The Milwaukee's participation includes the route from Chicago to Minneapolis including the Chicago-Milwaukee trains.

Basically the route is operating the Empire Builder and North Coast Hiawatha between Chicago and the Twin Cities — a set of trains between Milwaukee and Chicago; and if one wishes to stretch his imagination just a little, another pair of Amtrak trains runs over joint Milwaukee Road-Burlington Northern trackage between Hinckley, Minnesota and Duluth-Superior. However, the latter is handled by Burlington Northern Crews.

When Amtrak began operations, the Empire Builder was shifted from BN trackage to Milwaukee Road routing because of higher population centers along the Milwaukee. Originally only the Empire Builder operated each way daily, but the passenger load was too great. Frequently, a second section had to be operated in both directions to relieve the Empire Builder. Therefore, Amtrak added the "Hiawatha" between Chicago and Minneapolis on a daily basis. Three times a week the train operated to Seattle over the old Northern Pacific route, and the train became known as the North Coast Hiawatha thrice weekly, and the Twin Cities Hi the other four days. Eventually, the name "Twin Cities" was dropped, but as of October, 1977, the Twin Cities Hiawatha resumed daily service with Amfleet equipment.

The Chicago-Milwaukee service has been something else. At the start of the Amtrak service, the company operated three Chicago-Milwaukee trains each way daily, plus the Empire Builder. In fact, they even carried their old Milwaukee numbers of 9, 23, and 27 northbound; 12, 24 and 46 southbound. Numbers 9 and 46 were equipped with coaches only, while the other four trains carried what Amtrak called a Diner-lounge, actually Milwaukee Road lounges built in 1947-48.

Before 1971 was over, Amtrak had not only added trains to Minneapolis, but expanded the Chicago-Milwaukee service to seven trains in each direction. This was an increase of three trains daily in each direction. Two sets of these trains were domeliners operating a Milwaukee-St. Louis run: the Prairie State and the Abraham Lincoln. All trains carried at least snack or light meal and beverage service. Trains operated from Chicago at the following times:

Train #	Departure
321	9:15 am
9	12:01 pm The North Coast Hiawatha
323	1:30 pm Abraham Lincoln
7	3:00 pm Empire Builder
325	4:30 pm
327	6:30 pm
329	10:30 pm Prairie State

Trains operated from Milwaukee as follows:

Train #	Departure
320	6:10 am Prairie State
322	7:45 am
324	9:45 am
8	12:25 pm Empire Builder
10	2:15 pm North Coast Hiawatha
326	3:15 pm Abraham Lincoln
328	5:35 pm

The above schedules from Amtrak's November 14, 1971 System Timetable.

It was an excellent service in many ways, particularly in view of the services previously offered. By the end of 1972, Amtrak made some adjustments in the service offered. There were still seven trains in each direction, but No. 10 had been changed to a later departure from Minneapolis and departed Milwaukee at 5:20 P.M. The trains departed Milwaukee at 6:10 A.M., 7:20 A.M., 10:20 A.M., 1:20 P.M., 3:20 P.M., 5:20 P.M. and 7:20 P.M. Northbound departures from Chicago were: 8:30 A.M., 10:30 A.M., 1:30 P.M., 2:30 P.M., 4:30 P.M., 6:30 P.M. and 10:30 P.M. (Schedules from Amtrak timetable, September 10, 1972)

With the pooling of equipment, besides the Empire Builder, North Coast Hiawatha, Abe Lincoln

During the early days of Amtrak, some trains were made up entirely of Milwaukee Road equipment. This eastbound train is 2nd No. 32, the Empire Builder, heading toward Chicago with 12 cars looking for all the world like a Hiawatha sans a Super Dome and Sky-top parlor car. Later second section running of the Builder ceased with the addition of a "Hiawatha" train between Chicago and Minneapolis on a daily basis. However, the new train did not carry Milwaukee Road equipment as is shown here. (Russ Porter)

and Prairie State trains 321 and 328 also provided parlor car, food and beverage service. The other four trains provided coach, snack and refreshment service. The same general schedule prevailed through 1973.

All of the Chicago-Milwaukee trains were referred to as the Hiawatha service. And although the schedules were similar with seven through trains in each direction, the through St. Louis-Milwaukee train services were dropped.

During the first two years of Amtrak operation, the Milwaukee Road had increases in patronage. For the twelve months ended April 30, 1972, the Milwaukee carried 406,269 passengers. As of April 30, 1973, the number was 525,735 with a 29.4% increase. This compared very favorably with an Amtrak system wide increase of 6.6%. (Source: Annual Report, National Railroad Passenger Corporation, 1973, Washington, D.C., February, 1974, p. 59.)

Some major changes took place in early 1974. Although there were still seven trains in each di-

rection, ranging from 6:05 A.M. to 8:20 P.M. from Milwaukee and from 8:30 A.M. to 9:40 P.M. from Chicago, all meal, snack and beverage service was dropped from the Hiawatha Service trains. This arrangement continued until April, 1975 when there were a number of major changes made in the Hiawatha Services. A study was made by Amtrak, the State of Wisconsin and the City of Milwaukee which brought about the following changes:

The first southbound train in the morning departed Milwaukee at 7:20 A.M. daily except Sunday. Unfortunately, this move hurt many of the Milwaukee-Chicago commuters. The next train departed Milwaukee at 9:20 A.M. and another at 12:20 P.M., one hour later than the previous schedule.

Northbound the 8:30 A.M. train operated daily except Sunday, and the 10:30 P.M. train operated on Sunday only. Also the 8:20 P.M. departure from Milwaukee operated on Sunday only. With the new changes, Turboliners were also placed in service with one of the trains becoming a through

Hiawatha equipment ran on an "off again-on again" basis on numerous trains including the Chicago-Milwaukee territory. This eastbound train is arriving in Chicago with four Hiawatha cars numbered in the 600 series. (John H. Kuehl)

Milwaukee-Detroit train. The new schedule as of October 26, 1975 was as follows:

Northbound

Train #	Departure		
321	8:30 am	Turbo	Daily
9	10:30 am	North Coast	Daily
323	12:40 pm		Daily
7	2:30 pm	Emp. Builder	Daily
325	4:30 pm	Turbo	Daily
327	6:30 pm		Daily
329	10:30 pm		Sunday

Southbound

320	7:20 am	Turbo	Daily
322	9:20 am		Daily
324	11:45 am	Turbo	Daily
8	1:15 pm	Emp. Builder	Daily
326	3:20 pm		Daily
10	6:50 pm	North Coast	Daily
328	8:20 pm		Sunday

Source: Amtrak Timetables, October 26, 1975

Patronage increased about 10% from 1973 to 1974. During the period from January-December, 1975, the Chicago-Milwaukee patronage was 248,904 passengers. This was a decrease of 3% from the January-December, 1974 figure of 256,093 passengers. This was in part the reason for the reduction in train service between Chicago and Milwaukee in 1975.

Now here again we have an interesting thing happening. Service was reduced on the Milwaukee-Chicago run, but as we move into early 1976, patronage is increasing. During January, 1976, patronage was 16% over January, 1975, or 21,431 passengers as compared to 18,397 the year previous.

Turbos replaced all conventional Chicago-Milwaukee equipment before June 1, 1976. As part of the Chicago-Seattle schedule changes in the fall, trains 7, 8, 9 and 10 underwent adjustments between Chicago and Minneapolis, and this move affected some of the Chicago-Milwaukee Turbos as well.

The chapter on Amtrak will continue as long as Amtrak continues to operate over the Milwaukee Road. Although the chapter in this book must come to a close, it will be interesting to watch future developments take place. The Milwaukee Road has been maintaining an over 90% on-time dependability, which was what the Milwaukee Road was famous for over the years. The Milwaukee Road and Amtrak have been interesting operations to say the least.

Equipment shortages in 1976 found the 600 series car running between Chicago-Minneapolis and Duluth-Superior on the Empire Builder, North Coast Hiawatha and Arrowhead. Car 624 is awaiting the switch engine to place it in the consist of train 8, the Empire Builder, en route to Chicago in August, 1976. (Patrick C. Dorin)

Amtrak trains on Milwaukee Road trackage are not quite the same as the Hi's, Pioneer Limited and Fast Mail, but crowds still gather and patronage is now on the up-swing. Train 8 has stopped at Columbus, Wisconsin to load and unload passengers as well as exchange passengers with highway transportation to and from Madison, Wisconsin. (Patrick C. Dorin)

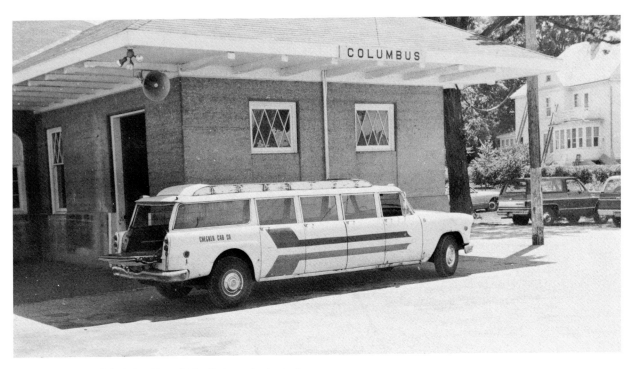

Madison's only rail link is this vehicle that meets Amtrak
trains at Columbus on a daily basis. (Patrick C. Dorin)

Amtrak train 8 pauses at the magnificent Milwaukee Road
depot in Milwaukee with a business car carrying the markers.
The head-end cars on the rear of train reflect increased express
and mail traffic. (Patrick C. Dorin)

Chicago-Milwaukee traffic is now handled by the Turboliners, such as this one between runs in the Milwaukee, Wisconsin depot. (Patrick C. Dorin)

On what could be the last regular assignment for Hiawatha coaches, the Arrowhead carried at least one 1948 coach during the summer months and early fall of 1976 between Minneapolis and Superior. Carrying the markers on this bright and sunny September day is car 630 with the Milwaukee colors of a bygone era on 763 at Cambridge, Minnesota.

FOR RESERVATIONS

For information and reservations phone the following Milwaukee Road stations:

Chicago, Ill. . . . . (312)   782-1520

Glenview, Ill. . . . . (312) PA 4-3110

Milwaukee, Wis. . . . . (414)   271-6150

Columbus, Wis. . . . . (414)   623-3700

Madison, Wis. . . . . (608)   255-4561

Portage, Wis. (608)   742-4200

Wisconsin Dells, Wis. . . . . (608)   254-8641

Tomah, Wis. . . . . (608)   372-4792

LaCrosse, Wis. . . . . (608)   782-7151

Winona, Minn. . . . . (507)   452-4062

Red Wing, Minn. . . . . (612)   388-2178

Minneapolis, Minn. . . . . (612)   332-3441

For information and reservations on Trains Nos. 31 and 32, 'phone any of the above offices or the Central Reservation Bureau, Burlington Northern: 800-328-1661 (toll free).

GENERAL INFORMATION

All times shown are local time.

Time shown in light numerals indicates a.m. **Time shown in dark numerals indicates p.m.**

The intercity trains show herein will be operated by the Chicago, Milwaukee, St. Paul and Pacific Railroad under contract for the National Railroad Passenger Corporation. The Chicago, Milwaukee, St. Paul and Pacific Railroad will not be responsible for errors in timetables or fares, inconvienence or damage resulting from delayed trains or failure to make connections. Schedules and equipment subject to change.

PASSENGER DEPARTMENT

THE MILWAUKEE ROAD

Chicago, Illinois 60606
Phone: (312) 236-7600

NATIONAL RAILROAD PASSENGER CORPORATION

TRAIN SCHEDULES

CHICAGO

MILWAUKEE

MINNEAPOLIS

PACIFIC NORTHWEST

THE INTERCITY TRAINS SHOWN HEREIN WILL BE OPERATED BY THE CHICAGO, MILWAUKEE, ST. PAUL AND PACIFIC RAILROAD AND BY THE BURLINGTON NORTHERN UNDER CONTRACT FOR THE NATIONAL RAILROAD PASSENGER CORPORATION.

First Amtrak summer time table published jointly by the Milwaukee Road and Amtrak.

READ DOWN   READ UP

No. 9 Daily	No. 23 Daily	No. 27 Daily	No. 31 Daily Empire Builder	Example	Miles from Chgo.	Central Time	Example	No. 32 Daily Empire Builder	No. 24 Daily	No. 12 Daily	No. 46 Daily
PM	PM	AM	AM			Union Station		PM	AM	PM	PM
7.25	4.20	9.40	10.45	Mon.	0	Lv Chicago (CMStP&P) .... Ar	Wed.	3.05	8.50	1.50	5.50
①7.48	①4.43	①10.03	①11.09	"	17	Lv Glenview .... Ar	"	①2.35	①8.24	①1.24	①5.24
8.55	5.50	11.10	12.15	"	85	Ar ⎰ Milwaukee ⎰ Lv	"	1.30	7.20	12.20	4.20
			12.20	"	85	Lv ⎱ Milwaukee ⎱ Ar	"	1.20			
PM	PM	AM	1.30	"	150	Ar Columbus Lv	"	12.08	AM	PM	PM
			1.40	"	0	Lv Columbus ♦ Bus ...... Ar	"	11.55			
			2.25	"	29	Ar Madison ⎰ Lv	"	11.10			
			12.30	"	0	Lv Madison ♦ Bus ...... Ar	"	1.00			
			1.15	"	29	Ar Columbus ⎰ Lv	"	12.15			
			1.30	"	150	Lv Columbus .... Ar	"	12.08			
			2.01	"	178	Lv Portage Lv	"	11.38			
			2.20	"	195	Lv Wisconsin Dells Lv	"	11.18			
			3.05	"	240	Lv Tomah Lv	"	10.35			
			3.50	"	281	Lv LaCrosse Lv	"	9.53			
			4.20	"	308	Lv Winona Lv	"	9.18			
			5.25	"	371	Lv Red Wing Lv	"	8.15			
			6.40	"	421	Ar Minneapolis (BN) Lv	"	7.10			
			7.25	"	421	Lv Minneapolis (BN) .... Ar	"	6.40			
			9.15	"	513	Lv Willmar Lv	"	4.40			
			f10.15	"	568	Lv Morris Lv	"	f3.45			
			11.10	Mon.	625	Lv Breckenridge Lv	"	2.50			
			12.20	Tue.	672	Lv Fargo Lv	"	1.45			
			1.40	"	750	Lv Grand Forks Lv	Wed.	12.01			
			3.30	"	839	Lv Devils Lake Lv	Tue.	10.25			
			5.40	"	957	Lv Minot Lv	"	8.25			
			7.45	"	1077	Ar ⎰ Williston (C.T.) ⎰ Lv	"	6.05			
			6.55	"	1077	Lv ⎱ Williston (M.T.) ⎱ Ar	"	4.55			
			8.40	"	1184	Lv Wolf Point Lv	"	3.13			
			9.25	"	1233	Lv Glasgow Lv	"	2.20			
			12.01	"	1386	Lv Havre Lv	"	11.45			
			1.45	"	1491	Lv Shelby Lv	"	9.55			
			②3.20	"	1562	Lv Glacier Park Lv	"	②8.20			
			②5.00	"	1618	Lv Belton Lv	"	②6.30			
			5.40	"	1641	Lv Whitefish Lv	"	5.55			
			7.35	"	1743	Lv Libby Lv	"	3.40			
			8.10	"	1761	Ar ⎰ Troy (M.T.) ⎰ Lv	"	3.15			
			7.10	"	1761	Lv ⎱ Troy (P.T.) ⎱ Ar	"	2.15			
			8.50	"	1827	Lv Sandpoint Lv	Tue.	12.30			
			10.10	Tue.	1894	Ar Spokane Lv	Mon.	11.20			
		7.00		Mon.	421	Lv Minneapolis (BN) .... Ar	Wed.			6.20	
		8.11		"	481	Lv St. Cloud Lv	"			4.55	
		9.17		"	551	Lv Staples Lv	"			3.45	
		10.18		"	613	Lv Detroit Lakes Lv	"			2.35	
		11.35		Mon.	666	Lv Fargo Lv	Wed.			1.30	
		1.30		Tue.	764	Lv Jamestown Lv	Tue.			11.42	
		3.05		"	866	Lv Bismarck Lv	"			9.55	
		3.20		"	871	Ar ⎰ Mandan (CT) ⎰ Lv	"			9.45	
		2.30		"	871	Lv ⎱ Mandan (MT) ⎱ Ar	"			8.35	
		4.25		"	971	Lv Dickinson Lv	"			6.55	
		6.35		"	1077	Lv Glendive Lv	"			4.55	
		7.50		"	1155	Lv Miles City Lv	"			3.26	
		8.47		"	1201	Lv Forsyth Lv	"			2.40	
		10.50		"	1302	Lv Billings Lv	"			1.05	
		12.50		"	1418	Lv Livingston Lv	"			11.05	
		1.35		"	1443	Lv Bozeman Lv	"			10.15	
		3.50		"	1537	Lv Butte Lv	"			7.50	
		6.00		"	1656	Lv Missoula Lv	"			5.35	
		7.35		"	1727	Ar ⎰ Paradise (MT) ⎰ Lv	"			3.47	
		6.38		"	1727	Lv ⎱ Paradise (PT) ⎱ Ar	"			2.45	
		f8.35		"	1846	Lv Sand Point Lv	"			f12.35	
		10.00		Tue.	1912	Ar Spokane Lv	Mon.			11.30	
			10.25	Tue.	1894	Lv Spokane .... Ar	Mon.	11.05			
			1.20	Wed.	2039	Lv Pasco Lv	"	8.20			
			3.15	"	2129	Lv Yakima Lv	"	6.30			
			4.10	"	2165	Lv Ellensburg Lv	"	5.25			
			6.50	"	2267	Lv East Auburn Lv	"	2.50			
			7.40	Wed.	2289	Ar Seattle Lv	Mon.	2.15			
			AM					PM			

(No. 27 column center: ↓ TRAIN NO. 25 (TRI-WEEKLY) ↓)
(No. 24 column center: ↑ TRAIN NO. 26 (TRI-WEEKLY) ↑)

Equipment

Nos. 31 and 32 Between Chicago and Seattle

Sleeping Cars
Roomettes
Double Bedrooms
Compartments

Slumbercoach

Reserved coach seats in Dome Coach between Chicago and points west of Minneapolis. Reserved coach seat charge (consult agent for details). Dome seats are not reserved.

Unreserved coach seats between Chicago and Minneapolis. Reserved coach seat charge not applicable locally between Chicago and Minneapolis and intermediate points.

Diner
Dome Lounge Car
Snack Refreshment Car

Nos. 27, 23, 24 and 12 Between Chicago and Milwaukee

Reclining seat coaches
Diner-Lounge

Nos. 9 and 46 Between Chicago and Milwaukee

Reclining seat coaches

Equipment

Train No. 25, North Coast Limited, tri-weekly from Minneapolis—Mondays, Wednesdays and Saturdays.

Train No. 26, North Coast Limited, tri-weekly from Seattle—Mondays, Wednesdays and Fridays.

One standard sleeper and one Dome Coach will be handled on Amtrak Trains Nos. 31 and 32 between Chicago and Minneapolis enroute to and from Seattle. All space reserved for points west of Minneapolis.

① Does not carry passengers locally between Chicago and Glenview. See Milwaukee Road suburban timetable.

② Stops at Glacier Park and Belton, eastern and western rail entrances to Glacier National Park, during the summer season.

f—Flag Stop.

♦ Amtrak tickets will be honored on bus.

Train 10, the Hiawatha "Amtrak style" races by Daytons Bluff
with a deadheading "Super Dome" en route to Chicago. The
"Hi" is two hours late this Sunday afternoon because of extreme
cold in Minnesota and the Dakotas. No one will ever forget
January, 1977 in those states.

Chapter 6
Freight Trains and Traffic

The backbone of any railroad is the freight service, and the Milwaukee Road is no exception. Freight service began immediately in 1850 hauling farm products, and the road is still, in many ways, a granger road. As we discovered with the passenger traffic innovations over the years, the same philosophy prevailed in much of the freight services. In 1937, for example, the Milwaukee placed a teletype system in operation between the various Chicago yards and the accounting office at Fullerton Avenue. This improved communications and car accounting tremendously, and the result was greater economies, faster freight deliveries and fewer lost cars.

Another innovation in 1937 was the rebuilding of cabooses. New cabooses were minus the cupola, but had bay-windows and were painted aluminum both inside and out. The bay-window caboose then set the stage for still others and eventually, most cupola cabooses were phased out. As time went on, the Milwaukee Road began painting their cabooses orange, a color that has prevailed to this day. Later new cabooses were delivered with yellow ends and now older "vans" are being repainted in that manner.

The company had many problems with merchandise freight handling. On September 30, 1940, they opened a new $500,000 receiving and transfer station at Galewood, Illinois (Chicago) to improve handling. All of the freight to and from connecting lines was then trucked instead of being handled across town in cars, which resulted in a savings of 24 hours on most of the merchandise handled through Chicago. Also at the same time, the company reduced their transcontinental freight schedule between Chicago and Seattle by 24 hours.

Other freight train improvements were made on overnight fast freights between Chicago and the Twin Cities, which resulted in a 15 per cent increase in traffic in early 1941. An additional train had to be added to handle the new traffic.

Aside from the cabooses earlier mentioned, the Milwaukee built much of their own freight equipment in their own shops, just as they did with the passenger quipment. One of the marks of Milwaukee Road-constructed equipment was the ribbing on car sides. This ribbing prevailed on not only passenger equipment, but the freight cars and cabooses as well. The Milwaukee Road, it can be said, built some of the finest equipment in America as they were truly master craftsmen. None of the car builders throughout the United States could really match the quality of much of the Milwaukee Road home built equipment.

World War II hit the Milwaukee Road quite hard, but she responded and began to move the traffic with great efficiency. Traffic in 1943 had increased 102% over the year 1939. According to Scandrett (Railway Age, December 11, 1943), the Milwaukee was able to handle the increased traffic by increasing the average load by 28 tons and the average car miles traveled by 59%. In other words, each carload was moving 59% more miles per day.

After the war, the Milwaukee Road immediately reduced its time freight schedule between Chicago, Twin Cities and the Pacific Northwest by another 24 hours. Merchandise freight began traveling in baggage cars on some passenger trains on an experimental basis, not only to relieve some freight trains but also to improve LCL service.

The company also worked hard to improve its freight car fleet. At the end of 1944, they owned 56,765 cars. At the end of 1949, the total stood at 58,714 cars.

By 1950, the Milwaukee had pretty well recovered from the effects of the war, and increased efforts were made to improve freight service in a most profound way. According to the Nov. 11, 1950 issue of Railway Age, the campaign began with a staff meeting held by President Kiley in Chicago in September of that year.

The meeting was held to bring out the gripes and problems of both traffic and operating officers, to isolate the impediments to good service and to come up with constructive solutions. The meeting was attended by both off-line and on-line traffic men, division superintendents, division engineers and master mechanics as well as system and regional staff men. The first day was exclusively the traffic department's, to put forth the needs of the customers. The second day brought the traffic and

operating people together, so that the former could put their case to the operating people, and the latter could air their difficulties. The final day the operating department considered what was needed in transportation, engineering and rolling stock to deliver the goods asked for.

Dieselization was rolling along, and at the same time improving the time schedules of freight trains. Bensenville yard went through a reconstruction process, as also would Pig's Eye yard in St. Paul and the Milwaukee, Wisconsin yards later.

The Milwaukee Road's subsidiary, The Milwaukee Motor Transportation Company became more intimately involved with freight train schedules, and by 1950 was operating over 1,567 miles on the Lines East.

In early 1955, the Milwaukee again cut 24 hours off the time schedule of freight 263 between Chicago and Tacoma, while schedule adjustments were made on a pair of freight trains between Chicago and Omaha. Dieselization was providing the company with the increased speed required for new and faster schedules.

The Milwaukee Road did not go into piggyback as rapidly as other roads. Instead, it elected to go into the container business. To be more specific, Flexi-vans. The Flexi-van was an operation whereby the body of the truck could be slid on to a turntable on a special flat car, without the highway wheels. Quite an innovation, and only the New York Central would take on the idea with equal, if not more, enthusiasm. Flexi-van flats averaged over 80,000 miles per year in freight service, and over 101,000 in mail service. A number of cars were equipped with steam lines for passenger train operation. By the mid-1970's the Flexi-van cars had been phased out of service in favor of piggyback, which started in earnest in the early 1960's. More about this later in this chapter.

A giant S-2 4-8-4 Northern teams up with an L-2 Mikado to power a fast time freight out of Bensenville yard. Note the superb track which made the "Milwaukee" famous. (The Milwaukee Road)

An eastbound freight moves off the Chicago & Milwaukee Division to the Techny Cutoff and Chicago & North Western trackage. Milwaukee Road freights to and from the old C&M division operate over North Western tracks to gain entrance to Bensenville yard. (The Milwaukee Road)

While on the C&NW, left hand running is the rule. This train is passing Des Plaines, Illinois on October 13, 1952 with 96 cars. (George-Paterson Collection)

Coming up the hill out of Milwaukee toward Chicago is a freight in the eastbound passing track. A passenger train is probably hot on its heels, and Lake Tower was held responsible for minimum delay to First Class trains. The year is 1951. (Russ Porter)

The Milwaukee's western terminal on the Missouri River is Council Bluffs, and at that point interchanges freight with a variety of railroads including the Union Pacific. On November 5, 1951, a transfer moves through Council Bluffs with a variety of freight traffic. (W. S. Kuba Collection)

An eastbound time freight moves through St. Paul Park,
Minnesota in late summer, 1954 with grain from South Dakota.
(W. S. Kuba Collection)

The Milwaukee Road refers to their local or way freights as
"Patrols." A westbound patrol approaches the small yard at
Lake Tower (south of Milwaukee) with just two hopper cars and
caboose during the summer of 1951. (Russ Porter)

The 1282 was assigned to patrol service out of Cedar Rapids, Iowa in May, 1939. (Paul Stringham)

A westbound freight operating on joint Burlington-Rock Island trackage (with the Milwaukee having rights) moves by the Clinton depot with a "Nahant Turn" (Savanna to Davenport) in August, 1954. (W. S. Kuba Collection)

Time freight 84 moves by the Roundout, Illinois interchange with the Elgin, Joliet & Eastern Railway with 83 cars on October 8, 1949. Despite dieselization, heavy steam power was still very much in use on the old C&M Division. (George-Paterson Collection)

L-2 Mikado No. 638 takes on coal at Milbank, South Dakota. (The Milwaukee Road)

0-6-0 switchers were quite functional and performed very well with extremely little praise. They did not achieve the fame of the streamlined Atlantics, but were every bit as important to the train operations of the Milwaukee. (Harold K. Vollrath Collection)

Type L-2 Mikado, No. 703 is shown at Savanna, Illinois in August, 1948. Built by Schenectady in 1914, the engine is equipped with foot boards for switching service. (Harold K. Vollrath Collection)

Type L-3 United States Railroad Administration heavy 2-8-2
at Bensenville, Illinois on June 7, 1935. (George-Paterson
Collection)

Type S-2 Northern at St. Paul, Minnesota with tender full of
coal for an outbound trip on April 10, 1938. (George-Paterson
Collection)

A rather obscure and little known branch of the Milwaukee Road extends from Iron Ridge to Fon du Lac, Wisconsin. Russ Porter has captured on film the type of power that serves the branch, two EMD switchers 647 and 642, as was the case a decade ago in 1968.

Fairbanks-Morse switch engine 701 idles coupled to a transfer caboose at North Milwaukee between switching assignments at the breweries. (Russ Porter)

Switcher 734 works a long string of freight cars at the North Milwaukee depot. The line to the right is the old Superior Division to Upper Michigan, while the line to the right is the old Northern Division to various Wisconsin points, such as Berlin, Oshkosh and Fond du Lac. (Russ Porter)

The line to Omaha and Kansas City played host to the "F" units in combinations of three, such as time freight 62 rounding the "S" curve at Paralta, Iowa in October, 1964. (W. S. Kuba Collection)

For many years freight trains on the main line between Chicago, Milwaukee and the Twin Cities were powered by matched "F" units. They added a bit of streamlining to freight trains and were among the most attractively designed diesel power ever built. (The Milwaukee Road)

Train 62 handled traffic from the Union Pacific. (W. S. Kuba Collection)

Baldwin No. 926 moves a work train eastbound south of Winona, Minnesota in May, 1971. (W. S. Kuba Collection)

Train 61 crosses the Mississippi River at Sabula, Iowa in October, 1963 with Union Pacific bound tonnage. (W. S. Kuba Collection)

Fairbank-Morse road-switcher No. 412 leads train 186 on the Ottumwa to Cedar Rapids patrol in February, 1964. (W. S. Kuba Collection)

Diesel units 596, 594, and 572 struggle up the steep grade into Cashton, Wisconsin on the Viroqua Branch on April 8, 1972. (W. S. Kuba Collection)

Some unusual road power on the Milwaukee Road were the Fairbanks-Morse units. Photographed at Savanna, Illinois by Russ Porter.

Three GP-30's and one F-7 lead train 61, bound for Omaha, into the CTC controlled siding at Covinton, Iowa in August, 1963. (W. S. Kuba Collection)

A Kansas City bound freight crosses the C&NW main line at Clinton, Iowa. The North Western bridge is in the background. (W. S. Kuba Collection)

Train 162 (now renumbered 260) is eastbound off the Dubuque line with meat on the head-end for eastern points. The train is a Sioux Falls-Bensenville run. (W. S. Kuba Collection)

Four GP-30's hustle a time freight over the DRI&NW track on the west bank of the Mississippi River at Pleasant Valley, Iowa on October 29, 1968. (Paul Stringham)

Train 62 rounds the curve at Sabula, Iowa on its run from Council Bluffs to Bensenville in August, 1968. (W. S. Kuba Collection)

An eastbound freight departs Dubuque en route to Savanna, Illinois. (W. S. Kuba Collection)

GP-40's 2026 and 2027 move train 251 out of Davenport, Iowa on the Fourth Sub of the Iowa Division en route to Kansas City. (Paul Stringham)

Train 61 west of Marion, Iowa in CTC territory on the Iowa Division in August, 1968. (W. S. Kuba Collection)

A westbound freight crosses the C&NW at Winona, Minnesota in April, 1972 en route to St. Paul yard. (W. S. Kuba Collection)

Train 262 (now renumbered 200) departs St. Paul yard in the early spring of 1974 with 108 cars for Chicago.

Four matched "F" units arrive at the St. Paul yard with transfer consisting of 72 cars from the Minneapolis side of the Missisippi River. It is a hot gloomy day in August, 1974 and the Burlington Northern units on the right are powering the Pacific Zip toward Seattle.

Not all unit grain trains operate solely in the winter. This westbound is taking empty cars for the grain-growing regions of the Dakotas, and has just crossed the Soo Line at Duplainville, Wisconsin. (The Milwaukee Road)

Train 210 (formerly 98) moves out of St. Paul with the All-Piggyback and auto-racks for the overnight run to Chicago. The westbound counterpart is 211 and they are two of the fastest freights on the Milwaukee.

Some patrols demand heavier power than others, and such is the case with the westbounds on the mainline between Milwaukee and St. Paul. These three units have cut off their train while the LaCrosse switch-engine works it over. The westbound here was being passed by train 7, the Empire Builder in May, 1976.

Train 200, the hottest of all Milwaukee Road freights, arrives at Bensenville, Illinois from Seattle-Tacoma with the red, white and blue leading the trio of power by tower B-17. (The Milwaukee Road)

The company has also operated mini-grain trains of 20 to 30 cars. This train is at Linwood, Iowa with 20 cars during the year 1974. Many of the trains operate to barge-loading facilities on the Mississippi River and then return to Iowa points for re-loading. (The Milwaukee Road)

A transfer arrives at St. Paul yard with a caboose on the head-end during the summer of 1976.

The Duluth trains operate with three or four GP-20's and happen to be the only Milwaukee Road trains that change direction — even though they continue in the same geographic direction. Symbol trains 610 and 611 operate between St. Paul and Duluth daily. Departing St. Paul the trains roll over the former North-ern Pacific, westbound to Hinckley, Minnesota. At that point, the train curves off the ex-NP on to the former Great Northern and becomes an eastbound train. The opposite takes place on trains running to St. Paul. This is train 610 at the Duluth yard.

During some winters, the Milwaukee Road places a snow plow on Burlington Northern trackage between St. Paul and Duluth. This car is at Forest Lake, Minnesota prior to being returned to St. Paul in the spring of 1975.

It is June, 1976 and a "so-called" Hastings and Dakota Extra is about to depart St. Paul yard with 186 cars.

Time freight 420 rolls by the Iron Mountain, Michigan station with a Milwaukee caboose on the head-end in August, 1976.

Pulpwood makes a major percentage of freight traffic in the Upper Peninsula of Michigan, and is handled in gondolas such as is shown here in train 420 at Iron Mountain.

Train 420 had a surprise package on the rear-end, a Chicago & North Western Railway caboose.

Diesel No. 40 was the Milwaukee's first freight power purchased in 1941 from Electro-Motive. Each unit was rated at 1350 horsepower and carried the classic grey and orange color scheme. (The Milwaukee Road)

No. 49A is shown here, in the current dress of motive power, on a train at Ladd, Illinois in November, 1969. This is on the branch which runs from Beloit, Wisconsin, south thru Rockford to Oglesby, Illinois and at one time was to be connected with Peoria. (Paul Stringham)

Extra 331 East is high-balling a grain train through Wauwatosa, Wisconsin during the winter of 1965. The Milwaukee
Road has operated solid grain trains from the Duluth-Superior
area during the winter season, when the lake carriers are
unable to sail. Much of this grain goes to the Buffalo, New York
area. (The Milwaukee Road)

Milwaukee 435 at Ladd, Illinois in October, 1966. Ladd was quite an important railroad junction where the Milwaukee connected with the CB&Q, NYC, C&NW and the LaSalle & Bureau County. (Paul Stringham)

The newest power in 1976 on the Milwaukee Road is the MP-15-AC's. These new switchers are now beginning to see service system wide. (The Milwaukee Road)

In addition to the rib-side passenger cars, the Milwaukee Road turned equally innovative (for greater strength) box cars that originally advertised the Hiawatha and Electrified Olympian. Rebuilds still carry big-as-ever lettering that few can miss. (The Milwaukee Road and Patrick C. Dorin)

Forty-foot box car constructed in 1961 by Pullman-Standard. (The Milwaukee Road)

Forty-foot car constructed in 1959 by Pullman. (The Milwaukee Road)

Forty-foot plug door box built by Pullman Standard in 1958. All freight cars are painted box car red with white lettering, with a few exceptions. (The Milwaukee Road)

Fifty-foot plug door box car with damage free interior equipment. Frequently used for hauling beer from the city of Milwaukee. (The Milwaukee Road)

Fifty-foot box car. (The Milwaukee Road)

An unusual box car with side doors between the truck centers and roof hatches. Rebuilt by the Milwaukee Road in 1957. (The Milwaukee Road)

123

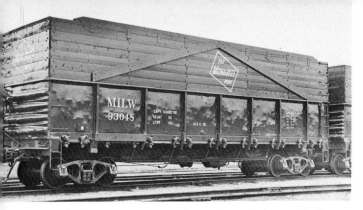

65-foot mill type gondola. (The Milwaukee Road)

Woodchip cars are operated not only in the Pacific Northwest, but also northern Wisconsin, Michigan and Minnesota. Some of this equipment is painted box car red with yellow lettering. (The Milwaukee Road)

50-foot flat car. (The Milwaukee Road)

A number of flat cars were rebuilt for piggyback service of automobiles between Detroit and the Pacific Northwest. (The Milwaukee Road)

An unusual innovation was Flex-van service. Operated in both freight and passenger service, the cars were capable of speeds up to 90 miles per hour. (The Milwaukee Road)

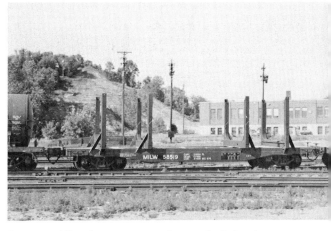

An unusual flat, these cars are seeing service in logging operations in Montana.

70-ton capacity covered hopper car. (The Milwaukee Road)

Triple hopper 70-ton capacity car. (The Milwaukee Road)

70-ton capacity air slide car. (The Milwaukee Road)

70-ton car with large block lettering. (The Milwaukee Road)

100-ton grain hopper proudly displays "America's Resourceful Railroad."

70-ton capacity open hopper used for ballast and revenue stone service. (The Milwaukee Road)

Ice refer 37469, Union Refrigerator Transit, was typical of the 40-foot cars in service for many years. The Milwaukee also worked with Dairy Shippers Dispatch for refer service.

Mechanical refer, 50 feet long with 60-ton capacity. (The Milwaukee Road)

Transfer caboose. (The Milwaukee Road)

Rib side caboose. (Russ Porter)

The last of the steel cupola cabooses had rather large windows. Some of these cars were still in operation in Washington during the mid-1970's. (Russ Porter)

The most modern Milwaukee Road cabooses ride on roller bearing caboose trucks and are equipped with cushion underframes. The car is on the tail end of a west bound extra departing St. Paul yard for Aberdeen, South Dakota.

The rib sides were dropped by the time these cabooses were built in 1956. Yet they were of similar design and rode on passenger car type trucks. (The Milwaukee Road)

Interior of 1956 cabooses. (The Milwaukee Road)

Chapter 7
The Lake Superior Iron Ore Districts

One of the more interesting sources of revenue for the Milwaukee has been its iron ore traffic. Most of this business is handled in a pool agreement with the Chicago & North Western Railway in the Upper Peninsula of Michigan. In this case, iron ore (and pelletized ores) are transported from mines and plants near Iron River, Iron Mountain and Champion to the C&NW ore terminal at Escanaba. (The Champion mine is now closed.) However, historically this has not always been the case, and the Milwaukee's ore operations have had a varied and colorful career.

The ore lines extend from the C&NW connection at Iron Mountain to Champion, a distance of about 55 miles. At Kelso there was a junction with a branch extending westward to Crystal Falls and Iron River, a distance of 38 miles. This section of line has now been abandoned. This basic system of trackage on the Michigan Iron Ranges has been about the same ever since their original construction during the time period 1887 to 1914.

The first line placed in service into the Iron Country was built by the Republic Branch Railroad Company in 1887. The line extended from the Menominee River (Iron Mountain) to Champion. That same year, the Republic Branch was consolidated with the Milwaukee and Northern Railroad. Six years later in 1893 the branch from Channing to Sidnaw, beyond the ore territory, was completed by the M&N. The M&N was then sold to the Chicago, Milwaukee and St. Paul Railway and the Milwaukee Road entered the iron ore picture — in 1893.

Further construction did not take place until 1900 when nearly seven miles of line was completed from Kelso on the Sidnaw line to Crystal Falls. The final segment from Crystal Falls to Iron River was completed in 1914 by the CM&StP. This basic system is still in operation to this day, as this is being written in early 1976, although some short sections of line have been abandoned.

When the original lines were constructed in the late 1880's, the iron ore traffic began almost immediately. However, the M&N lacked a port on either Lake Michigan or Superior through which to transfer their ore traffic from rail to Great Lakes ore carriers. In order to solve this problem, the M&N sought an agreement with the Soo Line Railroad, which had just constructed its Minneapolis-Sault Ste. Marie line through Pembine, Wisconsin and Gladstone, Michigan in 1887. Gladstone is situated on the Little Bay de Noc of Lake Michigan, not far from Escanaba. Pembine is located on the Milwaukee Road's north-south route just south of Iron Mountain.

An agreement was reached where iron ore traffic moved south on the M&N to Pembine and then via the Soo Line to Gladstone. The Soo Line constructed a timber ore dock 768 feet long at Gladstone for the new M&N's ore traffic. This arrangement continued until the Milwaukee Road constructed their own ore train yard and dock in Escanaba in 1901, at a cost of nearly $400,000. In 1906, the Company built a second ore dock. Both docks contained 240 pockets and were 1,440 feet long, pocket-to-pocket length. However, the railroad still did not have its own line to Escanaba.

In order to serve its Escanaba terminal, the Milwaukee Road obtained trackage rights with the Escanaba and Lake Superior Railroad. The E&LS connects with the Milwaukee Road at Channing. From 1901 through 1934, the Milwaukee sent its ore trains to its Escanaba docks via the E&LS. The year 1934 brought still another chapter in the history of the Milwaukee ore operations.

The depression was in full swing by 1931, and the C&NW and the Milwaukee both realized that it would be extremely inefficient to continue to compete with each other for ore traffic on the Menominee Range. A pool agreement was established in which revenue, costs, crews, facilities, motive power, ore cars and other equipment were shared on a percentage basis. From 1935 on, railroad operations on the Menominee Range were conducted as a "One Railroad Company" service. The Milwaukee Road docks and facilities were dismantled at Escanaba. In addition, service over the E&LS was discontinued.

With the exception of steam power, operations in the late 1960's and early 70's were much the same way as they were in 1935. Milwaukee Road power could be seen anywhere on either C&NW or Milwaukee Road trackage performing either mine switching or road service. Ore cars were pooled,

Smoking it up in grand style is Milwaukee Road "Mikado" No. 330 leading an eastbound ore extra over Chicago & North Western tracks at Florence, Wisconsin. The train is en route to the Escanaba docks from the Iron River District. The 46 car loaded train will fill out to 80 to 100 cars near Iron Mountain and continue to the Lake Michigan port. With the ore pool, C&NW and Milwaukee Road power were frequently seen on each others' trackage. Note the size of the 50-ton ore car as compared to the 70-ton cars following. (George-Paterson Collection)

and could be seen mixed in with C&NW and Lake Superior & Ishpeming Railroad ore cars. In fact, this is still true in the mid-1970's.

Nearly all ore trains originating on the Menominee Range are bound for Escanaba. The trains are assembled at the mines and run directly to the ore docks. Upon arrival at Escanaba, the trains go into a receiving yard west of the ore dock. When the cars are ready to be dumped, a switch crew takes part of the train and places it at the car dumper. From that point, an automatic train positioner sends the cut through the dumper three cars at a time. After dumping, the cars roll by gravity into a yard track for empty ore cars.

As of the present time, the Milwaukee Road's major ore train operation is to and from the Randville Mine. Milwaukee Road crews pick up empty ore trains from the C&NW at Iron Mountain, and

run the train through to the Randville pelletizing plant. There the cars are loaded and the Milwaukee Road moves the train back to Iron Mountain. From there the cars are forwarded to Escanaba via the C&NW for dumping and the process repeats itself.

Not all Milwaukee Road ore traffic is confined to the Menominee Range and the Escanaba ore docks. Certain companies ship ore or pellets by all-rail routes from one mine or plant directly to a steel company plant. One example is the shipments from Randville (location of the mine and pelletizing plant) to the St. Louis area. The pellets are shipped in 55 ton capacity hopper cars. This traffic usually travels south from Iron Mountain in solid ore trains, sometimes called unit trains, to Chicago where connections are made with other roads going to the St. Louis area.

A C&NW ten-wheeler switches four loaded ore cars at the James Mine at Caspian, Michigan on August 20, 1951. Both railroads participated in the revenue earned from all mines regardless of the railway serving the mine. Note the Chicago, Terra Haute & Southeastern Railway reporting marks on the first two Milwaukee Road ore cars. The author has not been able to learn precisely why such reporting marks were used, but two theories have been advanced. One is that a number of cars were purchased under CTH&SE financial arrangements, and the other was that the ore cars were sent south during the winter for coal hauling, and therefore the CTH&SE participated in the ownership. (Elmer Trelor)

The other ore traffic is Mesabi Range ores or pellets en route to Gary or Pittsburgh area mills. The Milwaukee Road connects with the Duluth, Missabe & Iron Range Railway at Duluth. The DM&IR delivers 100 car trains to the Milwaukee which then handles the train over its route from Duluth to Chicago, where again the train is interchanged with an eastern rail carrier. This particular traffic has been virtually non-existent for the company since ore boats have been operating to and from Two Harbors all winter long. The ore season is now virtually all year round for the DM&IR, as it also is with the Milwaukee Road with the movement of pellets to Escanaba during the entire year, although at the present time, ships do not load at that port during the winter.

Most of their ore or pellet traffic is handled in 24 foot, 70 ton capacity ore cars. A large percentage of these cars have been rebuilt with 18 inch extensions, and can be operated either on a conventional ore dock or through the C&NW's car dumper. Generally, Milwaukee ore cars are operated only in Upper Michigan. Rarely do they show up in Minnesota to or from the Duluth area.

The ore operations of the Milwaukee Road are as fascinating to watch as some of the heavy coal train movements in the east or far west. The colors of the ores range from black to blue and from red to brown, which makes the trains rather colorful at times. It appears that Milwaukee Road will continue to participate in ore traffic in the years to come, especially with the expansion of pelletizing plants in recent years. It could be said that the final chapter is a long way from being written, and that these iron ore railroad operations — unique to the Lake Superior Region — will be around for a long time to come for railroad men, rail fans, historians, geographers, economists and steel company men to observe, ponder and study.

The ground is shaking as Milwaukee "Mike" 350 leads C&NW No. 2457 with loaded ore cars for the Escanaba docks near the old Appleton Mine junction on the Menominee Range. (Harold K. Vollrath Collection)

Steam was replaced by Fairbanks-Morse 1600 horsepower "Baby Trainmasters" with six wheel trucks. The Milwaukee Road units were virtually identical to C&NW units and were used interchangeably all over the ore territory. The 550 is shown here between mine-run assignments at Iron River, Michigan in the early 1970's. (Patrick C. Dorin)

The bulk of the Milwaukee ore car fleet is made up of these 24-foot, 75-ton capacity cars with 18-inch extensions for pellet service. This photo shows the current 1976 lettering arrangement of white on box car red paint. The car was photographed at the Groveland mine and pelletizing plant north of Iron Mountain, Michigan on Milwaukee Road trackage. (Patrick C. Dorin)

As the mining industry shifts to pelletizing iron ore products, the need for switching and classification diminishes. However, it will not disappear completely. For example, sometimes a train load of pellets from the Groveland mine will have cars for two different destinations. These would be switched out at Iron Mountain. At other times, ore and/or pellets not in the pool service is interchanged to and from the C&NW at Iron Mountain — often another job for a switch crew. Still other reasons exist, such as the 751 moving a bad order car to the rip track at Iron Mountain during the winter of 1972. Ore trains now run all winter long in the Upper Peninsula of Michigan. (Patrick C. Dorin)

There are still ore cars without extensions, such as these two at the Escanaba and Lake Superior Railroad yards in Wells, Michigan. The reader may be interested to know that the Roundhouse Products "HO" gauge model ore cars are virtually identical to the Milwaukee Road cars. Note the square panels in the upper corners. In fact, the only difference is the hand brakes when compared to the model. These ore cars are different from the other rectangular ore cars found on the DM&IR, Soo Line and Burlington Northern. Some former Northern Pacific cars are close. (Patrick C. Dorin)

As ore cars without extensions are rebuilt, they have been repainted with a simpler lettering scheme, still box car red with white lettering and herald. The newer scheme includes the world famous "Milwaukee Road" insignia. The cars are operated in both pellet and natural ore service. This equipment was photographed at the C&NW's ore dock yard in Escanaba in the early 1970's. (Patrick C. Dorin)

During the summer of 1976, the Milwaukee Road operated an ore crew out of Iron Mountain for mine switching service. About noon, they would return to Iron Mountain with a short train, motive power being the 750. It is shown here returning to the freight house track to tie up for the morning. Upon completion of the morning duties, the crew would eat lunch and await the arrival of a complete train from the Chicago & North Western ore dock at Escanaba.

Upon arrival from Escanaba, the Milwaukee crew would take over the train and proceed north over Milwaukee trackage to the Groveland mine and pellet plant. The train is shown here with 3 C&NW Alco units, 100 C&NW ore cars and caboose.

133

Milwaukee ore operations are not confined to the C&NW dock service. All rail ore trains move south by the trainload. This photo shows a movement behind Milwaukee Road power with 139 loads of taconite pellets bound for Aliquippa, Pennsylvania. Other trains carry ore or pellets to Granite City, Illinois and other destinations. The photo was taken in the Upper Peninsula of Michigan on the route of the old Chippewa Hiawatha and Copper Country Limited. (The Milwaukee Road)

Chapter 8
Coal Trains From Indiana and Montana

Coal traffic has always been a part of the Milwaukee Road's freight traffic but it did not become a heavy coal train operator until the company leased the Chicago, Terre Haute & Southeastern Railroad in 1920. The CTH&SE operated a line from Chicago to Westport, Indiana, a distance of 374 miles, and passed through the southern Indiana coal fields. The lease was for 999 years, but the company has now purchased outright the entire railroad.

The acquisition of this line gave the Milwaukee access to the virtually unlimited coal supplies produced in the Indiana Bituminous fields. No longer did the road have to depend upon connecting carriers for its own coal supply.

The CTH&SE was incorporated in Indiana in November, 1910, taking over the properties of the Southern Indiana and the Chicago Southern railroads, both of which were in the hands of the receivers and were sold to the new company under foreclosure. In 1913 a lease with the Baltimore & Ohio Chicago Terminal was agreed to, giving the CTH&SE two terminal connections into Chicago.

Approximately 90% of the road's traffic was coal. This continued to be the mainstay of the Terre Haute Division for decades, and coal trains were a common sight. Coal continues to be important to the Terre Haute line with unit coal trains in operation to power plants in Indiana.

Coal is also handled from Montana with the Burlington Northern. In this movement, motive power, cars and cabooses are operated in a through train service to and from Montana to a power plant in Wisconsin. Fifty per cent of the time, the routing of this train alternates with one being interchanged to the Milwaukee Road at St. Paul and the next at Miles City, Montana. The result is great efficiency.

Along with this, the Milwaukee Road operates its only two wide vision cupola cabooses. Two such cabooses are operated on the pool coal train, and happen to be oddities on the Milwaukee with nearly all other cabooses being of the bay-window type.

Still another important unit train operation is the train with the "flip top" lid. This operation carries low-sulfur lignite from Gascoyne, North Dakota to the Big Stone power plant in North Eastern South Dakota, a distance of 350 miles. The name "flip top" comes from the use of a 100 ton coal gondola with a top lid that provides an effective top seal for the cars. Without the lid snow would accumulate in the cars during the empty movement. The lignite is loaded at a temperature of about 40°, which would melt the snow to form ice; thereby hampering unloading operations and reducing the carrying capacity of the cars. The lids are opened automatically as the train moves through the loading tipple at Gascoyne. As the train completes the loading process, the lids are locked shut. This also reduces the loss of the lignite, which is very light and has a tendency to blow out of the car.

For this operation, the Milwaukee operates two sets of equipment, each on a 48-hour turnaround, six days a week. It takes approximately 3 hours, 15 minutes to load the train, or about 30 cars per hour.

A special caboose, that looks like an extended transfer caboose, built to the same length as the 100 ton cars is operated on each train. They were designed to conform in length and other ways with the coal cars so as to act as an anchor for the trains' last load. The 56-foot cars mount a standard caboose body on a long underframe. These are the second set of special cabooses built for coal train service.

The Big Stone plant requires about 3 million tons of lignite annually, and is a combined venture of Montana Dakota Utilities, Northwestern Public Service Company and the Otter Tail Power Company.

Altogether, the Milwaukee Road handles about eight to nine million tons of coal annually. This amounts to about 20% of the total freight tonnage but less than 6% of the total revenues. Coal tonnages are expected to increase during the years ahead, and become an even more important commodity in the Milwaukee Road's freight traffic.

Coal was important during the days of steam as fuel was required system wide. To accomplish improved availability of coal, the Road secured the Chicago, Terre Haute and South Eastern Railroad, which served the Indiana coal country. This photo shows a transfer in the Chicago area approaching the Mayfair Crossing with engine fuel from Southern Indiana. (William A. Raia)

The Wisconsin Power unit coal train arrives at Dayton's Bluff yard with two Burlington Northern and two Milwaukee Road General Electric diesels. The unit train will travel over BN tracks from this point to the mine in Montana. The photo was taken during the summer of 1976.

Indiana coal is no longer mined for engine fuel, but for electric generating plants. Here cars are loaded at a mine near Latta, Indiana. (The Milwaukee Road)

Three GP-9's move an empty coal train southbound over the Wabash River bridge en route from Fayette to Latta on the Sixth Subdivision of the Illinois Division. This section of the railroad was once known as the Terre Haute Division. At the time of this writing, the line supports two time freights in each direction daily plus the daily round trip of the coal train. (The Milwaukee Road)

Wisconsin Power 100-ton capacity coal car.

Burlington Northern and Milwaukee Road not only pool motive power on the Wisconsin unit coal train, but also cabooses. Common on the Burlington Northern, cupola cabooses are rare on the Milwaukee. The 992301 is one of two such cars in the pool.

Some BN coal trains destined for the Twin Cities region are delivered to the Milwaukee Road for movement to the power plant receiving the coal. Consequently, it is not uncommon to see BN coal train power caboose hopping to and from the Milwaukee's St. Paul yard for a Montana coal train.

Extra 206 East heads into the morning sun as the train rolls across the prairie toward the Big Stone Power plant in eastern South Dakota. (The Milwaukee Road)

The most unusual operation is the Gascoyne, North Dakota-Big Stone coal train. About to begin loading, two SD-40-2's, an F-7 booster and another SD-40-2 lead a dynamometer car through the coal tipple. The overhead apparatus is for opening and closing the coal cars with the flip-top lids. (The Milwaukee Road)

Big Stone Power Company coal cars with the unusual cover. (Thrall Car Manufacturing Company)

Chapter 9
The Automatic Freight Classification Yards

Quite possibly the single most perplexing problem facing the railroad industry is freight car utilization. Freight equipment is expensive and all too frequently makes too few revenue trips during a year for an adequate return on the investment. Yet in order to provide service to thousands of shippers, a freight train may contain 100 cars from as many as 100 origins and going to as many as 100 destinations. This is where the complications come in, and the railroad industry has only begun to make inroads on this problem.

One of the ways to deal with the complexities of the multi-origin/destination freight train is the automatic classification yard. Such a yard can improve the speed of not only entire freight trains over the road, but of individual cars moving from origin to destination. Faster speeds mean better service for the customer and more revenue trips for each car, thereby providing a return on investment that encourages the construction of "push button" yards at strategic locations.

The Milwaukee Road recognized the value of such yards and invested heavily in three facilities at Chicago, Milwaukee and the Twin Cities. Each of these yards play an important part in Milwaukee Road freight service from Louisville, Kentucky to Tacoma, Washington. The first was completed in mid-1952 at Milwaukee, while the last was finished in August, 1956 at St. Paul.

The Milwaukee Yard

The Milwaukee yard was the first automatic facility in railroad history to combine both automatic switching and retarder speed control. The eight track 'A' yard receives trains arriving from the north and west. The hump yard, with 24 tracks ranging in capacity from about 20 to 60 cars, classifies outbound cars to the south and east. The yard is equipped with flood lights for night operation, paging and talk back speakers, a pneumatic tube system, teletypes for the handling of waybills and the transmission of other information for train make up, dragging equipment detectors, journal box oiling devices, automatic shunting of damaged cars onto repair tracks and many other innovations.

Cars to be classified are pushed in long strings to the crest of a graduated incline where they are uncoupled either singly or in blocks of cars according to destination. The operator in the control tower determines on which of the 24 classification tracks the next car or block of cars is to go and at what speed it must travel in order to go the required distance. By being able to line the switches for consecutive cuts of cars at a time, the operator is free to devote full attention to the degree of retardation each requires as it proceeds through the master retarder and one of the four secondary retarders. Loaded cars are controlled to leave the final retarders at no more than 4 miles per hour, and empty at correspondingly higher speeds. The grade of the tracks after leaving the final retarder is such that the cars gradually slow down approaching other cars on the same track.

The operator in the control tower sits before a console about the size of an office desk. The console displays the entire yard in miniature with a numbered button for each classification track. Projecting above it is an illuminated panel on which appears the numbers of the tracks for which the operator has set the switches in advance for the next five consecutive cuts of cars. Other sets of buttons permit the operator to change the speed of a car as it goes through each retarder. Also, the operator has a list of the cars to be switched including the car number, its contents, weight and destination. This list, originally sent from the yard office to the yardmaster, has been marked to indicate the track to which each car is to be directed. Another copy of this list is also sent to the switch foreman who supervises the uncoupling operation from a small office at the top of the hump.

At the time of this writing in early 1977, the facility has been serving the shipping public for 25 years.

Bensenville Yard – The Chicago Terminal

Seventeen miles west of Chicago is located the Milwaukee Road's largest automatic freight car classification yard, placed in service between July and November, 1953. The entire yard consists of 33 westbound classification tracks, and 37 eastbound

An aerial view of the Milwaukee hump yard, shown on the south bank of the river, center right in the photo. The Mitchell park flower domes can be seen upper right. The main line from Minneapolis on the left side, as well as the diesel house, lower left. The 35th St. Viaduct is in the foreground and the Muskego Yard stretches out across the top of the photo. (The Milwaukee Road)

classification and departure tracks for a total capacity of over 5000 cars. It was originally designed to classify 3600 cars in a 24 hour period.

The westbound departure yard has 5 tracks that are equipped with shove signals at the east end that indicate the number of car lengths of room at the west end.

The eastbound and westbound receiving yard consists of 20 tracks. Located at the entrance of this yard at both ends are illuminated yard track indicators. These indicators are operated by the yardmasters at both ends and control the movement of all trains entering the yard.

Trains arriving in Bensenville yard are checked and typed lists are sent to all who are involved in the switching operations. The lists show car numbers, contents, weight and destination as well as the track number they are to be switched to. The trains are pushed over the crest of the hump where a switchman uncouples the various cuts of cars that continue by gravity into the various tracks.

The switch foreman sits at a desk at track level on the hump, and lines up the routes for the different cuts into any of the 70 tracks. He can set up in advance in consecutive order the next five cuts of cars to be switched.

Half way down the grade there are two retarder towers, one on each side of the yard. Operators seated at desk type consoles control the speed of the cars into the classification tracks. On each console, there is a miniature diagram of the yard layout and an illuminated panel showing the next five routes set up by the switch foreman at the crest.

The yard is equipped with a paging and talk-back loud speaker system, telephone communication between offices, a pneumatic tube system to transmit way bills, train lists and switch lists as well as a flood-lighting system for night operations.

The yard also includes a complete locomotive servicing facility at the west end of the complex.

Another view of the Milwaukee yard facilities with the shops in the foreground. The Davies car repair yard can be seen to the east of the shops and the 35th St. viaduct. Lake Michigan can been seen at the top of the photo. (The Milwaukee Road)

Bensenville yard has approximately 125 miles of trackage, and is the largest yard on the Milwaukee Road.

St. Paul Yard

Located just southeast of St. Paul, this yard was completed in 1956. It has 35 classification tracks with 7 long receiving tracks and 6 departure tracks. Switch lists are sent to the switch foreman, located at the crest of the hump. There is a retarder tower located half way down the gravity grade, and the function here is the same as at Bensenville and Milwaukee. The only difference from the Milwaukee Yard is that the retarder operators are separated from the yard track switch control operators. Again, loaded cars are set to leave the final retarders at four miles per hour with the empty cars at correspondingly suitable higher speeds.

An interesting feature of the St. Paul yard is the cab signals in the diesel locomotives to facilitate the directing of their movements. There is also the usual communication system as described for Bensenville and Milwaukee, such as the talk back speakers, telephones, etc.

St. Paul yard also has an indicator, which shows the yardmaster at all times the number of cars on each track.

The yard also includes a large diesel locomotive servicing facility and a freight car repair yard at the west end.

The yard classifies trains both east and westbound to and from Chicago, the Pacific Northwest, Duluth, Austin, Minnesota, Kansas City, Omaha and scores of intermediate points.

The three push button automatic yards have reduced dead time for freight equipment.

Looking south across the shop area, one can see the Bluemound yard to the right, and the abandoned Rapid transit line of the Milwaukee Electric between the east-west expressway and the main line at the bottom of the photo. (The Milwaukee Road)

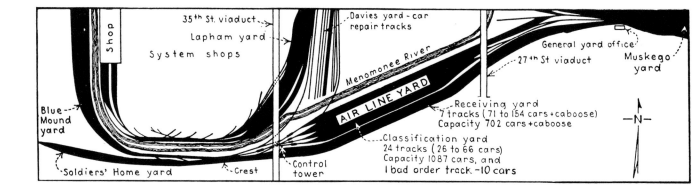

This view shows the Bensenville yards looking eastward. The
double track main line is to the left. (The Milwaukee Road)

Again looking east, the spot car repair shop is in the right
center, the hump right center, the yard offices near the same
location and the Chicago & North Western Proviso (Chicago
yards) and Butler (Milwaukee) main line at the lower right.
The arrival and departure yards are located between the hump
yard and the main line, which runs along the north side of the
entire complex. (The Milwaukee Road)

Container traffic is a new facet of business, and it too frequently
finds itself going through the classification routine at Bensenville. (The Milwaukee Road)

As cars reach the crest of the hump, a switchman uncouples the cars, "pulling the pin" as it is called. Bensenville yard often classifies more than 3600 cars per day. (The Milwaukee Road)

This view shows the east end of the yard with the piggyback terminal. O'Hare Airport can been seen in the upper right. (The Milwaukee Road)

Cars rolling down the Bensenville hump as viewed from the
yard tower. (The Milwaukee Road)

The car spot repair shop at Bensenville. (The Milwaukee Road)

The hump at St. Paul yard is located at the southern end with departure yards flanking both sides of the facility. The yard plays a key part in Twin Cities, Duluth, Southern Minnesota and transcontinental traffic. (The Milwaukee Road)

With the Mississippi River on the right, and Burlington Northern's Dayton's Bluff facility on the left, the Milwaukee's St. Paul yard stretches for several miles just southeast of downtown St. Paul. (The Milwaukee Road)

Cars roll down the hump at St. Paul yard. (The Milwaukee Road)

A pair of Baldwin switch engines working the hump at St. Paul shortly after its construction. Today, hump engines are made up of combinations of switching and road power in combinations of up to three units. The St. Paul sky line can be seen in the background. (The Milwaukee Road)

FACTS ABOUT THE MILWAUKEE ROAD'S AUTOMATIC YARDS

	Air Line Yard Milwaukee, Wis.	Bensenville Yard Chicago, Ill.	St. Paul Yard St. Paul, Minn.
A. Work Done at Yard	classifies eastbound and southbound cars	classifies cars to all destinations	classifies cars to all destinations
B. Date Placed in Service	May 1952	July 1953—37 tracks Nov. 1953—33 tracks	August 1956
C. Tracks and Capacity—Receiving	7 tracks 702 cars	20 tracks—1,575 cars	7 tracks— 843 cars
Classification	25 tracks 1,097 cars	70 tracks—5,311 cars	35 tracks—1,692 cars
Departure	directly from classification yard —— cars	5 tracks— 611 cars	6 tracks— 710 cars
	1,799 cars	7,497 cars	3,245 cars
D. Retarder Control Towers	1	2	1
E. Automatic Retarders—Master	1	1	1
Intermediate	■	4	2
Final	4	11	5
	5	16	8
F. Estimated Switching Capacity	2,400 cars per day	3,600 cars per day	2,400 cars per day
G. Miles of Track (In yards and operating facilities)	25 miles	125 miles	47 miles
H. Acreage (of yards and facilities)	60 acres	330 acres	120 acres
I. Approximate Cost of Project	$3,000,000	$5,200,000	$4,900,000

Issued by PUBLIC RELATIONS DEPARTMENT • 356 Union Station Building
Chicago 6, Illinois

Chapter 10
In Conclusion

In many ways, the Milwaukee Road has been an outstanding railroad and a number of its innovations have been covered in this small book. The politics and economics have been left for other writers. However, for all of the innovations and high speed train services, it is all too obvious in 1977 that the Milwaukee Road is ailing. It has been a marginal carrier at best with thin ice for profit figures. The answers to this, and the entire U.S. railroad problem will not come easily. It is impossible to speculate at this point what will happen to the Milwaukee Road. It has but two alternatives, either be absorbed by some larger healthier railroad or to create a new system of railroads using the transcon line as the focal point to begin rebuilding. One thing is certain, however, past plans by the U.S. government to consolidate railroad lines have been successful only to the point that the various companies agreed to disagree. Obviously, mergers are not the cure-all, especially if they create multiple traffic patterns (such as Penn Central) and management control breaks down because of a loss in freight car control. Railroad Geography Theory indicates that the more accurate freight car control is, the better the economic health of the railroad. In other words, unless a merger can improve car control it will not be successful.

Whatever its future, the Milwaukee Road will be remembered for many things. The "Hiawatha" fleet was one of the finest passenger train fleets in the world. Freight, passenger car and passenger car truck construction were far ahead of the entire railroad industry. Many of the techniques and concepts were adopted industry-wide. Motive power was another area of excellent operation. After other railroads had ceased to order the 4-4-2 steam locomotive, the Milwaukee Road was purchasing super Atlantics to power the "Hiawatha" at the same time the Burlington was opting for diesel powered articulated streamliners. During the mid to late 1930's, the Milwaukee outdid the competition in all ways between Chicago and the Twin Cities.

The Pioneer Limited, Fast Mail and the XL Special will be fondly recollected as will the super trains simply identified by number and operating on a 75 minute schedule between Chicago and Milwaukee. No doubt about it, the double track Chicago-Minneapolis speedway, touralux cars, friendly personnel and many other facets of its equipment, train service and physical plant all contributed to the Milwaukee Road being truly deserving of the motto

AMERICA'S RESOURCEFUL RAILROAD

Car-Scope went into service in late 1959. The new service grouped in a single office shipper service that had previously been performed by several departments. Its functions were:

1. To transmit daily, or oftener, to the Milwaukee's principal traffic representatives information concerning location of carload shipments to and from each agency territory.
2. To trace, and expedite carload shipments.
3. To give prompt handling to diversion and reconsignment orders.
4. To notify shippers and consignees if storms, failures or other causes delay cars en route, and notify them again when movement is resumed.
5. To keep track of and distribute all special purpose freight cars, so as to get maximum use for both shippers and railroad. In this case, Car-Scope is to work with local agencies to secure return loads for the special cars.

(Railway Age, p. 24, February 29, 1960)

The most exciting news in late 1963 was the XL-Special, which was the fastest run to the Pacific Northwest. The new trains (261 and 262) took only 55½ hours running time. The train was set up on the basis of having four GP-30's for power and a train weight of 3,000 tons. When the first XL-Special pulled out of Chicago on October 26, an office car and a dynamometer car were in the consist. Milwaukee operating and engineering men were there checking out the performance by securing a milepost-by-milepost diagram of the train with speed, drawbar pull and time indicated. The schedule was then modified slightly to take into consideration mountain grades, winter's extreme cold, crew changes, switching or pick-ups at Mil-

Train 69 races westward outside of Milwaukee en route from Chicago to St. Paul in December 1964. (Jim Scribbins)

waukee, St. Paul and Aberdeen as well as a rear-end St. Paul set out. The schedule called for a 2:30 P.M. departure from Chicago, Milwaukee at 5:00 P.M. and St. Paul at 1:30 A.M. Seven hours later it was due out of Aberdeen at 8:30 A.M. It was due into Seattle the next evening by 8:00 P.M.

To promote the new train schedule, as well as other time freights, the Milwaukee Road launched a "Red Vest" sales blitz in the Chicago area in April, 1964. The campaign was to inform all shippers of the faster service, and the results were very encouraging.

About the same time, train 262 received a new name, the Thunderhawk, and the two high speed freights began to endorse the reputation that the road had earned through its Hiawathas. Train 262 was slower than 261 by a few hours.

The XL-Special was not the only new train. In mid-1966, the Milwaukee launched the roaring 90's, trains 98 and 99 between Chicago and Twin Cities, all piggyback trains that operated overnight everynight. 99 was scheduled out of Chicago 6:30 P.M. with a 4:30 A.M. arrival in Minneapolis. Eastbound 98 departed Minneapolis at 4:45 P.M.

with a 3:00 A.M. arrival in Chicago. The result — fantastic!

Since then the Milwaukee Road has continuously upgraded their freight services. Run through trains are operated with the Union Pacific, with UP power and cabooses going through to Chicago. Schedules are co-ordinated for trains coming up from Louisville, going west and to various other points on the system. The purpose was to avoid the problems of having freight lay over as much as 24 hours because of a lack of connecting schedules.

The company is working continuously to upgrade its freight services system-wide. Piggyback and containers are continuing to grow, as well as coal traffic, which is covered in Chapter 8.

As we go to press, on December 19, 1977, the Milwaukee Road filed a voluntary petition for reorganization under Section 77 of the Federal Bankruptcy Act in the U.S. District Court in Chicago. It is extremely difficult to predict what the outcome or the future of the Milwaukee Road is at this time.

Symbol Freight 223, enroute from Bensenville to Council Bluffs, travels westward over the Iowa Division about one mile west of Herndon, Iowa with Union Pacific bound tonnage on Oct. 19, 1977. (Milwaukee Road Photo by Barbara Scribbins)

APPENDICES

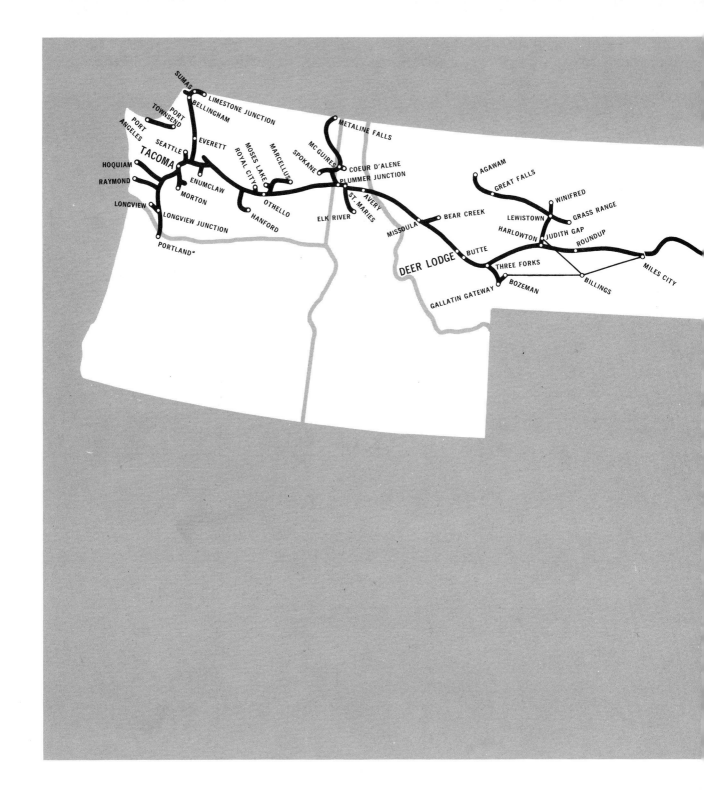

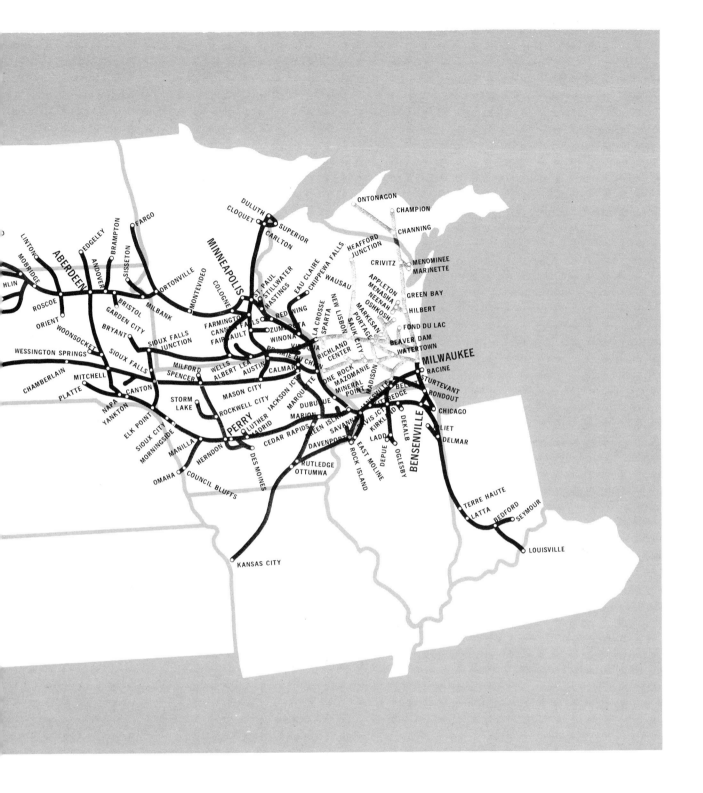

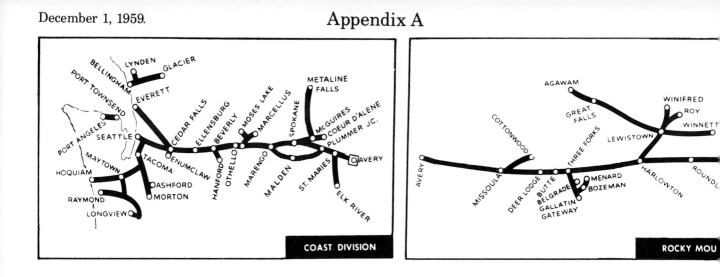

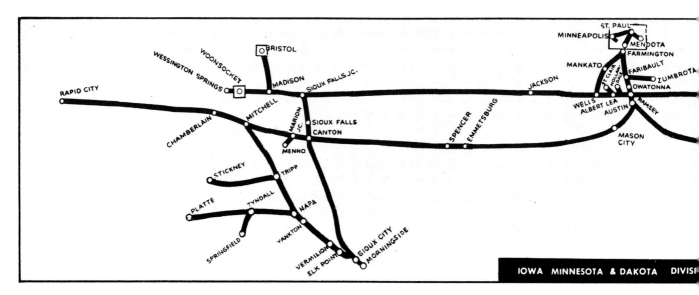

DIVISIONAL CHANGES
from 1959 to 1976.

THE

MILWAUKEE

ROAD'S

OPERATING

DIVISIONS

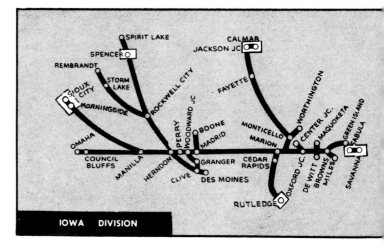

Note: In the individual divisional maps, lines and towns
enclosed in box [image] are not part of the divisions with which they are shown.

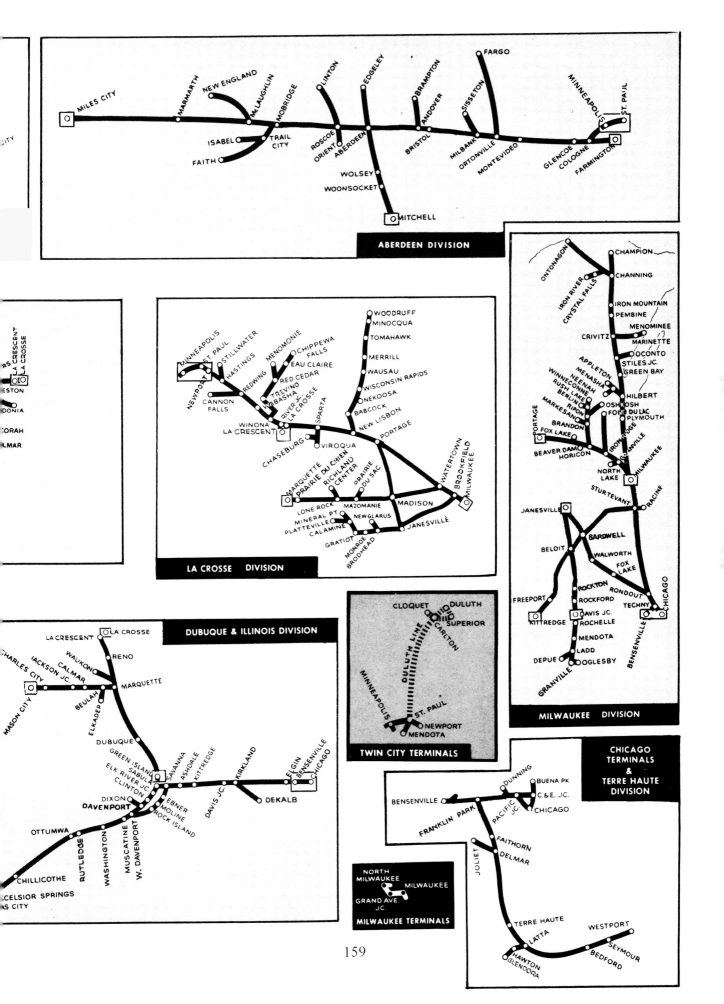

ABERDEEN DIVISION

LA CROSSE DIVISION

DUBUQUE & ILLINOIS DIVISION

TWIN CITY TERMINALS

MILWAUKEE DIVISION

CHICAGO TERMINALS & TERRE HAUTE DIVISION

MILWAUKEE TERMINALS

1973

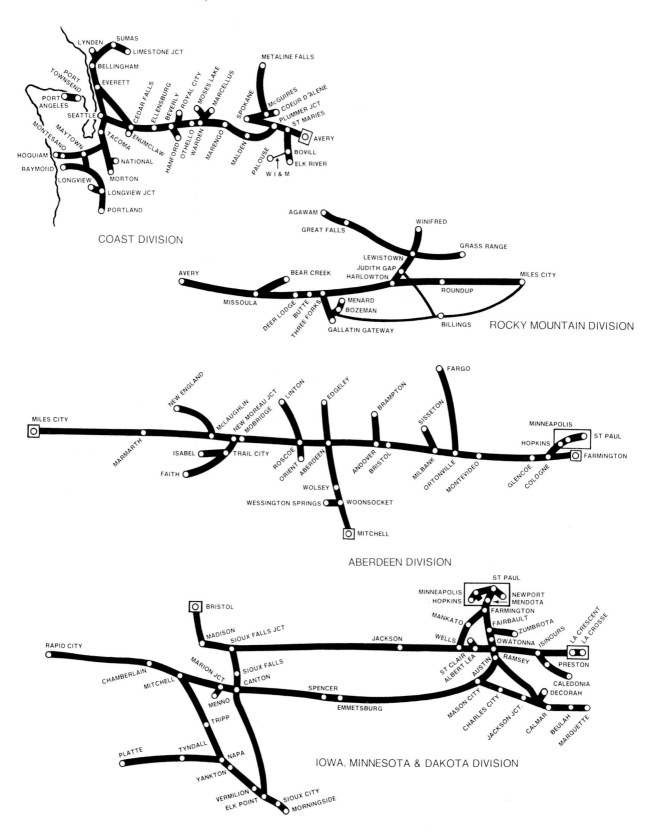

COAST DIVISION

ROCKY MOUNTAIN DIVISION

ABERDEEN DIVISION

IOWA, MINNESOTA & DAKOTA DIVISION

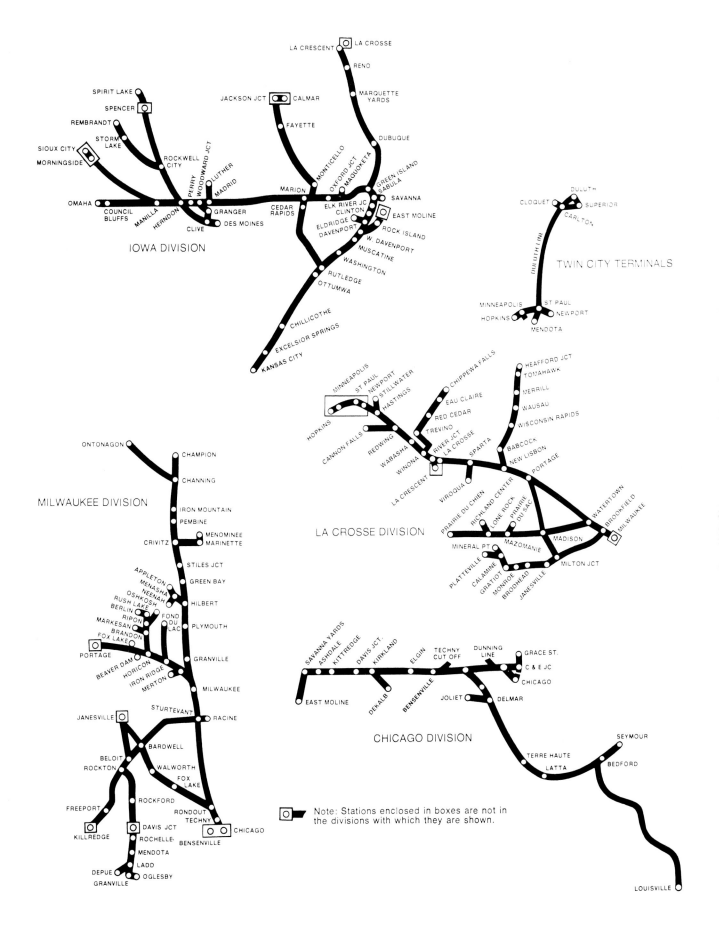

IOWA DIVISION

LA CRESCENT · LA CROSSE
RENO
JACKSON JCT · CALMAR
MARQUETTE YARDS
FAYETTE
DUBUQUE
SPIRIT LAKE
SPENCER
REMBRANDT
STORM LAKE
SIOUX CITY
MORNINGSIDE
ROCKWELL CITY
WOODWARD JCT
LUTHER
MADRID
MONTICELLO
OXFORD JCT
CLINTON
MAQUOKETA
GREEN ISLAND
SABULA
SAVANNA
MARION
OMAHA
COUNCIL BLUFFS
MANILLA
HERNDON
PERRY
GRANGER
CLIVE
DES MOINES
CEDAR RAPIDS
ELK RIVER JC
ELDRIDGE
DAVENPORT
EAST MOLINE
ROCK ISLAND
W. DAVENPORT
MUSCATINE
WASHINGTON
RUTLEDGE
OTTUMWA
CHILLICOTHE
EXCELSIOR SPRINGS
KANSAS CITY

TWIN CITY TERMINALS

DULUTH
CLOQUET · SUPERIOR
CARLTON
DULUTH LINE
MINNEAPOLIS
HOPKINS
ST PAUL
NEWPORT
MENDOTA

LA CROSSE DIVISION

MINNEAPOLIS
ST PAUL
NEWPORT
STILLWATER
HASTINGS
CHIPPEWA FALLS
EAU CLAIRE
HEAFFORD JCT
TOMAHAWK
MERRILL
WAUSAU
WISCONSIN RAPIDS
HOPKINS
CANNON FALLS
REDWING
WABASHA
WINONA
RED CEDAR
TREVINO
RIVER JCT
LA CROSSE
SPARTA
BABCOCK
NEW LISBON
PORTAGE
LA CRESCENT
VIROQUA
PRAIRIE DU CHIEN
RICHLAND CENTER
LONE ROCK
PRAIRIE DU SAC
WATERTOWN
BROOKFIELD
MILWAUKEE
MINERAL PT
MAZOMANIE
MADISON
PLATTEVILLE
CALAMINE
GRATIOT
MONROE
BRODHEAD
JANESVILLE
MILTON JCT

MILWAUKEE DIVISION

ONTONAGON
CHAMPION
CHANNING
IRON MOUNTAIN
PEMBINE
MENOMINEE
MARINETTE
CRIVITZ
STILES JCT
GREEN BAY
APPLETON
MENASHA
NEENAH
OSHKOSH
RUSH LAKE
BERLIN
RIPON
MARKESAN
BRANDON
FOX LAKE
PORTAGE
BEAVER DAM
HORICON
IRON RIDGE
MERTON
HILBERT
FOND DU LAC
PLYMOUTH
GRANVILLE
MILWAUKEE
STURTEVANT
JANESVILLE
BARDWELL
RACINE
BELOIT
ROCKTON
WALWORTH
FOX LAKE
FREEPORT
ROCKFORD
RONDOUT
TECHNY
KILLREDGE
DAVIS JCT
ROCHELLE
MENDOTA
LADD
DEPUE
GRANVILLE
OGLESBY
CHICAGO
BENSENVILLE

CHICAGO DIVISION

SAVANNA YARDS
ASHDALE
KITTREDGE
DAVIS JCT
KIRKLAND
ELGIN
TECHNY CUT OFF
DUNNING LINE
GRACE ST.
C & E JC
CHICAGO
EAST MOLINE
DEKALB
BENSENVILLE
JOLIET
DELMAR
SEYMOUR
TERRE HAUTE
LATTA
BEDFORD
LOUISVILLE

Note: Stations enclosed in boxes are not in the divisions with which they are shown.

161

THE MILWAUKEE ROAD

OPERATIONS PLANNING
JANUARY 1, 1976

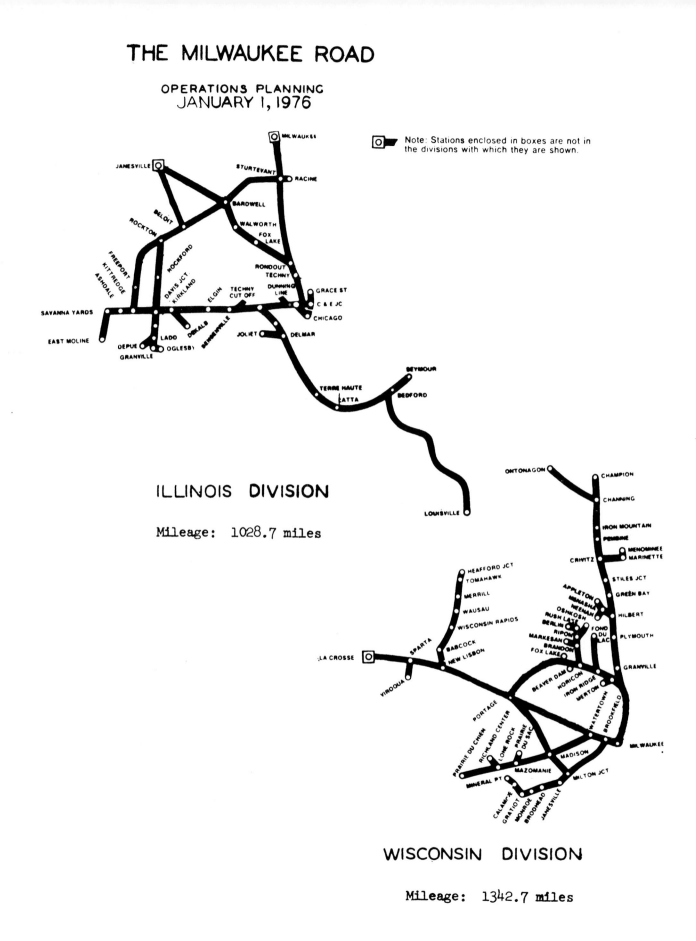

Note: Stations enclosed in boxes are not in the divisions with which they are shown.

ILLINOIS DIVISION

Mileage: 1028.7 miles

WISCONSIN DIVISION

Mileage: 1342.7 miles

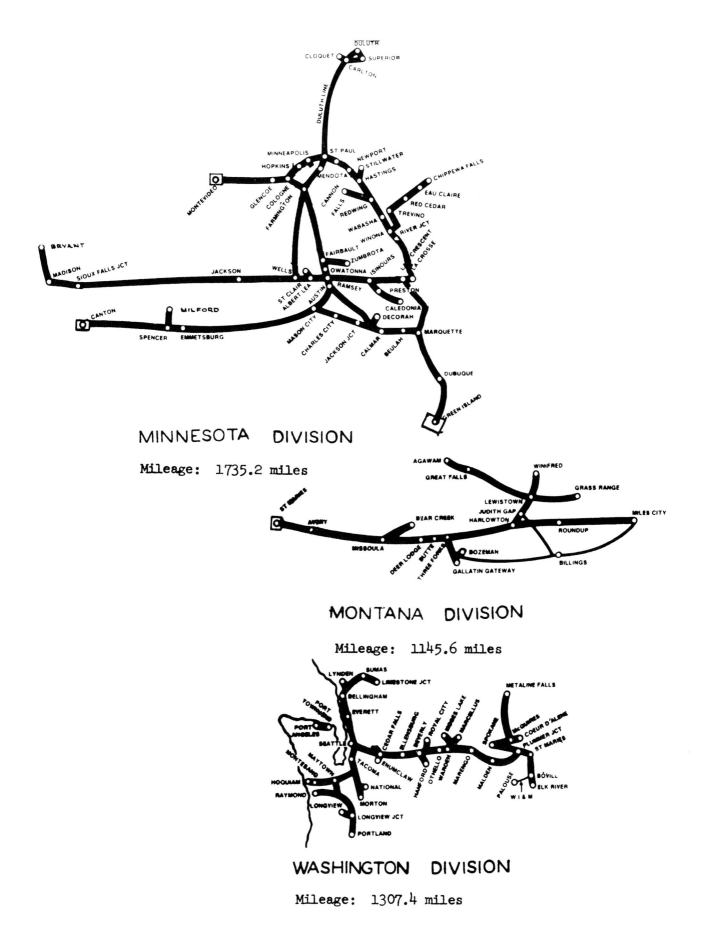

MINNESOTA DIVISION

Mileage: 1735.2 miles

MONTANA DIVISION

Mileage: 1145.6 miles

WASHINGTON DIVISION

Mileage: 1307.4 miles

Appendix B
HIAWATHA TRAIN SCHEDULES
January 20, 1952.

12

All Passenger Trains powered by Diesel or Electric Locomotives

Chicago-Milwaukee-St. Paul-Minneapolis

READ DOWN   READ UP

THE PIONEER LIMITED	THE COLUMBIAN	OLYMPIAN HIAWATHA	AFTERNOON HIAWATHA	MORNING HIAWATHA			Miles from Chgo.	Table 1 *Central Time*	Altitude	OLYMPIAN HIAWATHA	MORNING HIAWATHA	AFTERNOON HIAWATHA	AFTERNOON HIAWATHA	THE FAST MAIL	THE COLUMBIAN	THE PIONEER LIMITED
57	1	17	15	101	5	55				16	6	58-14	100	56	18	4
Daily	Daily	Daily	Daily	Daily	Daily	Daily				Daily	Daily	Daily	Daily	Daily	Daily	Daily
	PM	PM	PM	PM	AM	AM		*Union Station*		PM	PM	PM	PM	AM	AM	AM
	11.15	10.00	3.30	1.00	10.30	1.30	0	Lv **Chicago** ‖ I........ Ar	583	1.45	2.40	9.40	7.15	6.20	8.45	8.00
							3	Lv Western Ave......... Ar	609					6.12		
	①11.45	⑥10.30		⑱ 1.23			24	Lv Deerfield............ Lv	687			⑯ 9.04		㉑ 5.37	⑩ 8.10	㉑ 7.10
							62	Lv **Sturtevant** I....... Lv	726							
								Milwaukee River								
	12.45	11.30	4.45	2.15	11.45	3.05	85	Ar **Milwaukee** ‖ I {Lv	595	12.25	1.25	8.10	6.00	4.35	7.05	6.10
	12.55	11.40	4.45	2.15	11.52	3.25	90	Lv } *LaCrosse & River Div.* { Lv		12.20	1.20	7.40	5.55	4.22	6.55	6.00
								Lv Wauwatosa *Mil.County Inst's.* Ar	655			⑨			⑬	
								Menomonie River								
							95	Lv Elm Grove........... Lv	749			⑨			⑬	
							99	Lv **Brookfield**......... Lv	836			⑨			⑬	
							102	Lv Duplainville▲........ Lv	859			⑨			⑬	
						f 3.54	105	Lv Pewaukee.......... Lv	858			⑨			⑬	
							110	Lv Hartland.......... Lv	931			⑨			⑬	
						f 4.05	113	Lv Nashotah.......... Lv	943			⑨			⑬	
							115	Lv Okauchee▲......... Lv	904			⑨			⑬	
	1.30				12.26	4.22	118	Lv **Oconomowoc** I...... Lv	871			6.50			⑮ 6.06	
							124	Lv Ixonia........... Lv	874			⑨			⑬	
								Rock River								
		12.30			12.42	5.10	131	Lv **Watertown** I *(Fox Farms)*.. Lv	826			6.30	5.10	3.22	5.51	
								Rock River								
							135	Lv Richwood......... Lv	842			f 6.19			⑬	
						5.24	141	Lv Reeseville........ Lv	829			f 6.12			⑬	
						5.34	146	Lv Astico.......... Lv	830			f 6.04			⑬	
								Crawfish River								
		12.50			1.03	5.50	150	Lv **Columbus**........ Lv	850		12.20	5.59		⑨ 2.54	⑭ 5.27	
						5.57	153	Lv Fall River........ Lv	877			f 5.50			⑬	
						6.05	159	Lv Doylestown....... Lv	955			f 5.43			⑬	
						6.15	164	Lv Rio........... Lv	934			f 5.36			⑬	
						6.23	169	Lv Wyocena........ Lv	831			f 5.28			⑬	
	2.27	1.26	6.05	3.32	1.30	6.43	178	Ar **Portage** ‖ I...... Lv	817	10.53	11.56	5.15	4.32	2.24	4.58	4.15
	10.30	10.30	2.00	2.00			0	Lv *Madison*........ Ar				6.00	8.35	8.35	8.35	
	11.45	11.45	3.15	3.15			37	Ar *Portage*........ Lv				4.40	7.10	7.10	7.10	
	2.37	1.46	6.07	3.34	1.33	7.01	178	Ar **Portage** ‖ I...... Lv	817	10.51	11.54	5.05	4.30	2.14	4.48	4.08
	⑫ 2.54			⑤	1.50	7.28	195	Lv **Wisconsin Dells**...... Lv	899		④	4.46		③ 1.55	⑬	
								Wisconsin River								
						7.38	203	Lv Lyndon *(Military Ridge)*.. Lv	904			4.33			⑬	
						7.58	214	Lv Mauston.......... Lv	885			4.18			⑬	
				2.07	2.20	8.21	221	Ar } **New Lisbon** ‖ I....... { Lv	894			4.05	3.57	1.28	4.05	
	3.34	2.34		4.11	2.20	8.21		Lv {				3.25	3.57	1.28	4.05	
	3.34	2.34		4.11	2.20	8.35	227	Lv Camp Douglas...... Lv	934			3.14		1.06	⑬	
						8.43	233	Lv Oakdale.......... Lv	954							
	4.00				2.37	9.01	240	Lv **Tomah** I....... Lv	962			2.59		12.53	⑬	
						9.05	243	Lv Tunnel City ○▲..... Lv	1060			f 2.45			⑬	
						9.15	250	Lv Camp McCoy...... Lv	903			2.34		⑫12.37	⑬	
	⑲ 4.35	3.12			2.55	9.30	256	Lv **Sparta** I........ Lv	793		10.55	2.26		12.30	3.23	
						9.37	263	Lv Rockland▲........ Lv	765			2.12			⑬	
						9.44	266	Lv Bangor.......... Lv	747			2.12				
						9.55	271	Lv West Salem....... Lv	746			2.05			⑬	
	5.15	3.45	7.28	5.00	3.27	10.15	281	Ar **La Crosse** ‖ I *(Game Pres.)* Lv	653	9.28	10.33	1.53	3.08	12.02	2.55	2.25
	5.20	3.55	7.33	5.05	3.32	10.25		Lv/ *Mississippi River* \Ar		9.23	10.28	1.43	3.03	11.50	2.45	2.20
							283	Lv Bridge Switch, Minn.▲.. Lv	663							
							284	Lv River Jct.▲....... Lv	653							
					⑩10.36		289	Lv Dresbach▲....... Lv	680			f 1.19				
					10.43		291	Lv Dakota.......... Lv	664			f 1.15				
					⑩10.54		299	Lv Lamoille▲........ Lv	664			f 1.04				
					②11.01		304	Lv Homer▲......... Lv	666			f 12.57				
	⑬ 5.55	4.32	8.00	5.34	4.04	11.12	308	Lv **Winona** I *(Garvin Hts.St.Pk.)* Lv	664	8.48	9.59	12.50	2.34	11.14	2.01	1.41
						11.22	314	Lv Minnesota City▲.... Lv	683			12.34				
						11.32	324	Lv Minneiska▲....... Lv	679			f 12.20				
						11.38	328	Lv Weaver▲......... Lv	678			12.15				
						11.48	335	Lv Kellogg.......... Lv	706			12.07				
								Zumbro River								
		5.10			4.36	12.01	341	Lv **Wabasha** ‖ I....... Lv	713			11.59		10.30	.. ⑪	
							343	Lv Read's Landing▲..... Lv	698							
		5.24			4.50	12.18	354	Lv **Lake City** I *Lake Pepin*.... Lv	718			11.40		10.14	.. ⑦	
						12.26	360	Lv Frontenac▲....... Lv	726			11.31				
	⑬ 7.00	5.52		6.32	5.13	12.43	371	Lv **Red Wing** I *(Training School)* Lv	691		9.03	11.18	1.38	9.53	12.51	
		6.17			5.35	1.10	391	Lv **Hastings** I *(Spiral Bridge)*.. Lv	713			10.51		9.26	.. ⑪	
								Mississippi River								
							402	Lv Newport▲........ Lv	756							
	8.00	6.55	9.45	7.15	6.05	1.50	410	Ar **St. Paul** ‖ I *(State Capitol)* .{ Lv	722	7.10	8.25	10.25	1.00	9.00	12.01	11.59
	8.10	7.15	9.45	7.18	6.15	2.10		Lv } *Union Station* {		7.05	8.12	10.00	12.55	8.45	11.37	11.35
								Mississippi River								
	8.40	7.40	10.15	7.45	6.45	2.35	421	Ar **Minneapolis** ‖ I *(Flour Mills)* Lv	844	6.25	7.50	9.35	12.30	8.20	10.50	11.10
	AM	AM	PM	PM	PM	AM		*Milwaukee Road Station*		PM	PM	PM	PM	PM	PM	PM

Left margin note:
Fast Mail and Express Train. Leaves Chicago, daily, 9.00 p.m., stops at Milwaukee, Portage, New Lisbon, Camp Douglas, Sparta, La Crosse, Winona, Red Wing, arrives St. Paul 5.40 a.m., Minneapolis 6.15 a.m. Does not carry passengers or baggage.

Column notes (under AFTERNOON HIAWATHA 15 and 101): *Does not carry checked baggage or dogs*

For equipment see pages 8 to 11.

Reference Marks for Table 1:

‖ Meals.   ○ Tunnels.

* Daily.

† Except Sunday.

I U. S. Mail box at station.

▲ Non-agency station.

f Stops on signal to leave or take passengers.

① Stops to take revenue passengers for New Lisbon or beyond.

② Stops on signal to take passengers.

③ Stops to leave revenue passengers from north of New Lisbon, La Crosse and beyond, or take revenue passengers for Milwaukee or beyond.

④ Connection made by bus to Portage.

⑤ Connection made by bus at Portage.

⑦ Stops to leave revenue passengers from St. Paul and west.

⑧ Stops to take revenue passengers for points beyond New Lisbon.

⑨ Stops to leave revenue passengers from points between Woodruff-Minocqua and New Lisbon.

⑩ Stops to leave revenue passengers from St. Paul or beyond.

⑪ Stops to leave revenue passengers from Mobridge or beyond.

⑫ Stops to leave revenue passengers from Milwaukee or beyond or take revenue passengers for St. Paul or beyond.

⑬ Stops to leave revenue passengers from Aberdeen and west.

⑭ Stops to leave revenue passengers from the Twin Cities or beyond or take revenue passengers for Milwaukee or Chicago.

⑮ Stops to leave revenue passengers from Twin Cities or beyond and Sunday only to take revenue passengers for Chicago.

⑯ Stops to leave revenue passengers from Milwaukee or beyond.

⑰ Stops Mondays only.

⑱ Stops to take revenue passengers for beyond Milwaukee.

⑲ Stops to take passengers for Winona or beyond.

⑳ Stops to leave revenue passengers from beyond Milwaukee.

NOTE: 1952 Schedules selected to show all six Hiawatha Schedules as well as other trains, such as the Columbian and Arrow.

164

St. Paul-Minneapolis-Butte-Spokane-Seattle-Tacoma

Table 2 — Central Time

READ DOWN — READ UP

THE COLUMBIAN 101 -5 PM	OLYMPIAN HIAWATHA 17 Daily PM	15 Daily PM	Miles from Chgo.	Station	Alti-tude	OLYMPIAN HIAWATHA 16 Daily PM	THE COLUMBIAN 18 Daily AM	6 PM
				Union Station				
* 1.00	10 00	3 30	0	Lv **Chicago** ‖ꭓ............Ar	583	1 45	8.45	* 2 40
2.15	11.40	4 45	85	Lv **Milwaukee** ‖ꭓ..........Ar	595	12 20	6.55	1 20
7.15	6.55	9 45	410	Ar ⎱ **St. Paul** ‖ꭓ......... ⎰ Lv	722	7.10	12.01	8.25
7.18	7.15	9.45		Lv ⎰ ⎱ Ar		7.05	11 37	8.12
7.45	7.40	10.15	421	Ar ⎱ **Minneapolis** ‖ꭓ..... ⎰ Lv	844	6.25	10.50	7.50
8.30	7.55	10.25		Lv ⎰ (U. of Minn.)....... ⎱ Ar		6.20	10.35	7.15
f 8.50			429	Lv St. Louis Park........Lv	917			f 6.38
f 8.52			432	Lv **Hopkins**...........Lv	920			f 6.30
f 8.59			439	Lv Chanhassen▲..........Lv	955			6.13
f 9.07			448	Lv Augusta▲............Lv	970			f 5.55
f 9.13			453	Lv Cologne▲............Lv	947			5.45
f 9.18			457	Lv Bongards▲...........Lv	980			5.38
③ 9.41			461	Lv **Norwood**..........Lv	990			5.30
f 9.47			466	Lv Plato.............Lv	995			5.10
10.09	9.22		472	Lv **Glencoe**..........Lv	1004		9.29	5.00
			477	Lv Sumter▲............Lv	1030			f 4.43
f10.21			482	Lv Brownton...........Lv	1018			4.36
f10.28			489	Lv Stewart............Lv	1063			4.23
f10.35			495	Lv Buffalo Lake.........Lv	1073			4.11
10.45			500	Lv Hector............Lv	1080			f 4.01
f11.01			509	Lv Bird Island..........Lv	1089			3.45
11.15	10.09		514	Lv Olivia............Lv	1082		8.44	3.25
f11.22			519	Lv Danube............Lv	1083			3.10
f11.28			525	Lv Renville............Lv	1067			3.00
f11.36			532	Lv Sacred Heart.........Lv	1060			2.44
12.20	⑤1038		541	Lv **Granite Falls**.......Lv	938		⑦8.13	2.20
				(Boulders of Granite)				
f12.28			549	Lv Wegdahl...........Lv	932			2.02
1.00	11.00	12.55	554	Lv **Montevideo**ꭓ.......Lv	924	4.07	7.57	1.55
				(Camp Release Monu't)				
......			560	Lv North Watson▲........Lv	950			
1.27			570	Lv Milan.............Lv	1092			1.27
1.42	⑤1125		578	Lv **Appleton**.........Lv	1005		⑤7.18	1.18
1.52			585	Lv Correll............Lv	976			12.43
2.02			594	Lv Odessa............Lv	958			12.32
2.12	11.51		600	Lv **Ortonville, Minn.**....Lv	988		6.54	12.23
				(Big Stone Lake)				
2.26			601	Lv Big Stone City, S. D...Lv	1000			12.15
2.59	12.09		611	Lv **Milbank** (Old Windmill) Lv	1142		6.38	12.01
3.12			618	Lv Twin Brooks.........Lv	1256			11.40
3.29			626	Lv Marvin▲...........Lv	1651		⑥1128	11.18
3.51			633	Lv Summit...........Lv	1998			11.18
4.01			641	Lv Ortley............Lv	1859			11.08
4.16			646	Lv Waubay...........Lv	1811			11.00
4.39	1.03		657	Lv **Webster**..........Lv	1841		5.45	10.44
4.47			663	Lv Holmquist..........Lv	1804			f10.32
5.07	1.18		668	Lv **Bristol**..........Lv	1777		5.27	10.25
5.22			678	Lv Andover...........Lv	1475			9.58
5.36			688	Lv Groton............Lv	1303			9.43
f 5.45			694	Lv James............Lv	1300			f 9.33
				James River				
f 5.52			699	Lv Bath.............Lv	1300			f 9.27
* 6.10	2.00	3.18	707	Ar ⎱ **Aberdeen** ‖ꭓ..... ⎰ Lv	1299	1.30	4.35	* 9.15
	2.15	3.33		⎰ ⎱ Ar		1.15	4.20	
......	2.35		720	Lv Mina.............Lv	1431		4.02	
	f 2.43		728	Lv Craven▲...........Lv	1486		f 3.53	
	2.55		733	Lv Ipswich............Lv	1532		3.48	
	f 3.03		741	Lv Beebe▲...........Lv	1732		f 3.34	
	3 20		749	Lv **Roscoe**..........Lv	1826		3.20	
	3 32		757	Lv Gretna▲...........Lv	1916		f 2.55	
	3.45		764	Lv Bowdle............Lv	1993		2.45	
	4.02		777	Lv Java Junction........Lv	2045		2.25	
	4.18		784	Lv Selby............Lv	1877		2.10	
	f 4.26		792	Lv Sitka▲............Lv	1766		f 1.55	
	4.45		796	Lv Glenham...........Lv	1679		1.50	
	5.00	5.05	805	Ar ⎱ **Mobridge** (C.T.) ‖ ..⎰ Lv	1653	11.40	1.35	
	4.10	4.10		Lv ⎰ (Trans.Mo.Div) Mt.T. ⎱ Ar		10.35	12.25	
				Missouri River				
	4.25		817	Lv Wakpala...........Lv	1633			
				Standing Rock Indian Reser.				
	4.37		828	Lv Mahto▲...........Lv	1805			
	5.01		835	Lv **McLaughlin**........Lv	1998		11.38	
			844	Lv Cadillac▲..........Lv	2022			
	5.18		851	Lv Walker▲...........Lv	2162			
	5.40		864	Lv **McIntosh**.........Lv	2272		11.01	
			873	Lv Watauga...........Lv	2248		10.47	
	6.05		882	Lv Morristown..........Lv	2240		10.37	
			886	Lv Keldron▲...........Lv	2355		10.30	
	6.22		895	Lv Thunder Hawk........Lv	2579		10.20	
	6.32	⑤5.43	904	Lv Lemmon, S. D.......Lv	2567	⑦8.56	10.09	
			910	Lv Petrel, N. D.▲.......Lv	2555			
AM	PM	AM		*Continued in table 3*		PM	AM	PM

Table 3 — Mountain Time

READ DOWN — READ UP

THE COLUMBIAN 17 Daily PM	OLYMPIAN HIAWATHA 15 Daily AM	Miles from Chgo.	Station	Alti-tude	OLYMPIAN HIAWATHA 16 Daily PM	THE COLUMBIAN 18 Daily AM
			Continued from table 2			
		910	Lv Petrel, N. D.▲.......Lv	2555		
		913	Lv White Butte, S. D.▲...Lv	2495		9.52
		919	Lv Haynes, N. D........Lv	2540		9.45
7.25	6.10	927	Lv **Hettinger**.........Ar	2668	8.31	9.35
7.35		936	Lv Bucyrus...........Lv	2778		f 9.20
7.45		945	Lv Reeder............Lv	2810		9.09
8.03		951	Lv Gascoyne...........Lv	2759		f 8.59
8.09		955	Lv Scranton...........Lv	2773		8.55
		959	Lv Buffalo Springs▲......Lv	2850		8.48
8.35	①6.49	967	Lv **Bowman**.........Lv	2958	①7.46	8.40
		975	Lv Griffin▲...........Lv	3048		
8.55		981	Lv Rhame............Lv	3184		8.21
		986	Lv Ives▲............Lv	3087		
			Little Mo. River			
9.30	7.20	995	Ar ⎱ **Marmarth** ‖..... ⎰ Lv	2709	7.18	8.03
9.50	7.23		Lv ⎰ ⎱ Ar		7.15	7.53
		1010	Lv Kingmont, Mont.▲.....Lv	3028		
10.25		1015	Lv Baker (Gas Wells).....Lv	2934		7.21
f10.40		1028	Lv Plevna (Lignite Beds)...Lv	2757		f 7.01
		1036	Lv Westmore▲.........Lv	2648		
f11 01		1044	Lv Ismay............Lv	2524		f 6.44
		1051	Lv Lacomb▲..........Lv	2453		
f11 20		1059	Lv Mildred...........Lv	2362		f 6.27
		1067	Lv Whitney▲..........Lv	2274		
		1073	Lv Bluffport▲..........Lv	2245		f 6.02
f11.44		1080	Lv **Terry**..........Lv	2247		
			Yellowstone River			
		1086	Lv Calypso▲...........Lv	2240		
		1093	Lv Susan▲...........Lv	2256		
		1099	Lv Bonfield...........Lv	2280		
		1105	Lv Kinsey............Lv	2310		
		1112	Lv Tusler▲...........Lv	2339		
12.45	9.40	1119	Lv **MILES CITY**ꭓ......Lv	2358	5.05	5.20
			Tongue River			
			Fort Keogh			
			Yellowstone River			
		1127	Lv Paragon▲ (Moss Agates)..Lv	2406		
		1135	Lv Sheffield▲..........Lv	2418		
		1145	Lv Thurlow...........Lv	2468		
f 1.19		1152	Lv Carterville..........Lv	2495		f 4.29
		1159	Lv Orinoco▲...........Lv	2509		
1.33		1164	Lv **Forsyth**..........Lv	2535		4.18
1.55		1182	Lv Vananda...........Lv	2705		3.58
		1191	Lv Ahles▲...........Lv	2881		
		1197	Lv Thebes▲...........Lv	2919		
2.23		1204	Lv Ingomar...........Lv	3040		3.30
		1210	Lv Galbraith▲.........Lv	3111		
2.35		1214	Lv Sumatra...........Lv	3186		3.15
		1224	Lv Bascom▲..........Lv	2937		
			Musselshell River			
3.05		1231	Lv **Melstone** ‖........Lv	2897		2.55
		1237	Lv Keene▲...........Lv	2946		
		1243	Lv Musselshell.........Lv	2997		
		1249	Lv Delphia▲..........Lv	3053		
		1258	Lv Gage▲............Lv	3128		
4.00	11.50	1265	Lv **Roundup** (Coal) ꭓ....Lv	3188	2.35	2.16
			Bull Mountains			
		1275	Lv Elso▲............Lv	3274		
		1282	Lv Bundy▲...........Lv	3348		
②4.31		1290	Lv Lavina............Lv	3443	②1.45	
4.42		1296	Lv Slayton▲..........Lv	3514		1.38
		1298	Lv Burgoyne▲.........Lv	3540		
			Musselshell River			
②4.57		1306	Lv Ryegate (Crazy Mts.)...Lv	3641		1.24
		1312	Lv Barber▲...........Lv	3727		
		1320	Lv Shawmut..........Lv	3857		
		1327	Lv Winnecook▲........Lv	4008		
5.45	1.00	1335	Ar **Harlowton** ‖ꭓ......Lv	4167	1.30	12.50
* 9.25		1399	Lv **Lewiston**ꭓ........Ar	3926		9.00
2.00		1535	Ar **Great Falls**ꭓ......Lv	3337		* 4 35
* 4.35		1535	Lv **Great Falls**ꭓ......Ar	3337		2.00
9.00		1399	Ar **Lewiston**ꭓ........Lv	3926		* 9.25
			Rocky Mountain Division			
6.00	1.05	1335	Lv **Harlowton** ‖ꭓ......Ar	4167	1.25	12.36
			Musselshell River			
6.18		1348	Lv Two Dot...........Lv	4434		12.18
6.37		1360	Lv Martinsdale.........Lv	4822		12.01
f 6.44		1364	Lv Groveland▲.........Lv	5010		f11.47
f 6.55		1371	Lv Lennep...........Lv	5239		f11.47
f 7.05		1377	Lv Bruno▲...........Lv	5510		f11.37
AM	PM		*Continued in table 4*		PM	PM

Electrified — Belt Mountain (Rocky Mountain Division)

Explanation of Reference Marks for Tables 2 and 3.

* Daily.

‖ Meals.

▲ Non-agency station.

ꭓ U. S. Mail box at station or on platform.

f Stops on signal to take or leave passengers.

① Will stop to leave or take passengers from or for Aberdeen or beyond or leave or take passengers from or for Miles City or beyond.

② Stops to leave or take revenue passengers from or for Aberdeen or beyond and to leave or take from or for Harlowton or beyond.

③ Stops daily except Saturday.

④ Stops to leave or take revenue passengers from or for Minneapolis or beyond and to leave or take revenue passengers from or for Spokane or beyond.

⑤ Stops daily except Sunday.

⑦ Stops at North Granite Falls to let off revenue passengers from Spokane and west or take revenue passengers for Minneapolis or beyond.

Mixed trains provide service. Consult Agent for details.

For equipment see pages 8 to 11.

All Passenger Trains powered by Diesel or Electric Locomotives

Three Forks-Butte-Missoula-Spokane-Seattle-Tacoma

Table 4 — Mountain Time

17 Daily	15 Daily	Miles from Chgo.	Station	Altitude	16 Daily	18 Daily
AM	PM		*Continued from table 3*		AM	PM
f 7.05		1377	Lv Bruno (Mt. T.)▲	5510		f11.37
f 7.15		1381	Lv Loweth▲	5799		f11.28
			Summit Big Belt Mts.			
f 7.22		1385	Lv Hamen▲	5585		f11.19
7.36		1393	Lv **Ringling**	5304		11.06
f 7.41		1396	Lv **Moyne**▲ O	5219		f10.58
f 7.51		1403	Lv Sixteen▲	4979		f10.43
			Montana Canyon			
f805		1411	Lv Francis▲	4647		f10.27
f812		1415	Lv Nathan▲	4454		f10.15
f816		1417	Lv Maudlow▲	4398		f10.15
f825		1423	Lv Deer Park▲ O	4200		f10.05
f834		1428	Lv Cardinal▲	4038		f954
			Montana Canyon			
8.40		1430	Lv **Lombard** O	3984		9.50
			Missouri River			
f844		1434	Lv Barron▲	3969		f942
f855		1441	Lv Eustis▲	4014		f931
			Jefferson, Madison, Gallatin Rivers, forming Missouri River			
9.08	3.57	1450	Ar Three Forks‖I	4062	10.30	9.20
12.15	5.35	1482	Ar} **Gallatin Gateway**	4906	(7)7.35	(7)7.30
(7)	(7)		*Entrance*			
7.35	2.30		Lv} **Yellowstone Park**		12.15	1050
9.18	3.59	1450	Lv Three Forks‖I	4062	10.28	9.15
f 9.26		1456	Lv Willow Creek▲	4142		f 9.05
f 9.33		1463	Lv Sappington▲	4183		f 8.58
			Jefferson Canyon			
			Lewis and Clark Cavern State Pk.			
f 9.55		1475	Lv Jefferson Island▲	4259		f 8.41
			Jefferson River			
f10.10		1484	Lv Piedmont▲	4355		f 8.29
f10.31		1494	Lv Cedric (Vigilante Trail)▲	5178		f 8.14
f10.45		1498	Lv Grace▲ O	5664		f 8.05
f11.04		1505	Lv Donald▲	6315		f 7.54
			Continental Divide, Pipestone Pass Tunnel, Length 2,290 ft. Alt. 6,347			
		1506	Lv Penfield▲	6285		
f11.17		1512	Lv Janney▲	5869		f 7.43
f11.24		1515	Lv Newcomb▲	5613		f 7.36
11.44	5.48	1522	Ar} **BUTTE**‖I	5538	8.38	7.23
11.55	5.51		Lv} (Copper Mines)		8.35	7.10
		1528	Lv **Silver Bow**▲			
f12.07		1530	Lv Dawson▲	5287		f 6.47
f12.29		1544	Lv Morel▲	4875		f 6.23
f12.39		1554	Lv Sinclair▲	4675		f 6.10
1.05	6.55	1562	Lv **Deer Lodge**‖I	4508	7.35	6.00
			(State Penitentiary)			
f 1.16		1573	Lv Garrison▲ O	4315		f 5.30
f 1.25		1580	Lv Gold Creek▲	4180		f 5.20
			Hell Gate River			
f 1.31		1586	Lv Haskell▲	4060		f 5.13
f 1.39		1593	Lv **Drummond**	3959		f 5.06
f 1.53		1603	Lv Bearmouth▲ O	3805		f 4.50
f 2.05		1613	Lv Ravenna▲ O	3658		f 4.38
f 2.12		1619	Lv Iris▲			f 4.30
f 2.19		1625	Lv Clinton▲	3446		f 4.23
f 2.27		1630	Lv Thelma▲	3335		f 4.16
f 2.34		1635	Lv Bonner Jct.▲	3280		f 4.10
2.50	8.19	1641	Lv **Missoula** I	3183	5.50	4.01
			(University of Montana)			
f 3.01		1650	Lv Primrose▲	3073		f 3.44
f 3.10		1657	Lv Frenchtown▲	3027		f 3.35
f 3.27		1667	Lv Soudan▲	3030		f 3.27
3.38		1672	Lv **Alberton**‖I	3040		f 3.20
f 3.47		1679	Lv Cyr▲ O	2987		f 3.09
f 3.58		1688	Lv Tarkio▲	2927		f 2.59
f 4.08		1695	Lv Cobden▲	2825		f 2.50
f 4.19		1703	Lv Superior▲	2727		f 2.40
f 4.27		1710	Lv Ashmore▲	2677		f 2.31
f 4.36		1716	Lv **St. Regis**▲	2678		f 2.22
			St. Regis River			
f 4.47		1722	Lv Foraker▲	2750		f 2.10
f 4.58		1726	Lv Drexel▲	2860		f 2.01
f 5.08		1730	Lv Henderson▲	2980		f 1.51
		1732	Lv DeBorgia▲	3035		
f 5.18		1735	Lv **Haugan** (Govt. Nursery)▲	3124		f 1.45
f 5.30		1741	Lv Saltese▲	3476		f 1.34
f 5.38		1745	Lv Bryson▲	3758		f 1.27
f 5.49		1749	Lv East Portal, Mont.▲	4152		f 1.17
			Summit Bitter Root Mts.			
			St. Paul Pass Tunnel, lgth. 8,733 ft.			
f 5.56		1751	Lv Roland, Idaho▲	4153		f 1.11
f 6.07		1756	Lv Adair▲	3775		f 1.01
f 6.19		1760	Lv Falcon▲ O	3420		f12.51
f 6.30		1766	Lv Kyle▲	3002		f12.40
f 6.38		1769	Lv Stetson▲	2728		f12.33
			St. Joe River			
6.53 PM	11.30 PM	1773	Ar **Avery**‖I	2492	2.25 AM	12.25 PM
			Mountain Time			

Vertical markings for Table 4: THE COLUMBIAN, OLYMPIAN HIAWATHA, Belt Mountains, Rocky Mountains, Clark Fork River, Bitter Root Mts., ELECTRIFIED.

GRAND COULEE DAM — Daily Bus Service between Spokane and Coulee Dam

Explanation of Reference Marks for Tables 4 and 5

* Daily.
‖ Meals.
O Tunnels.
I U.S. Mail box at station or on platform.
▲ Non-agency station.
f Stops on signal to take or leave passengers.
①Stops on signal to take or leave revenue passengers.
⑤Stops to leave or take revenue passengers from or east or take or leave revenue passengers for or from Seattle and west.
⑦During Yellowstone Park Season only.
Light numerals indicate a.m.
Dark numerals indicate p.m.

Table 5 — Pacific Time

17 Daily	15 Daily	Miles from Chgo.	Station	Altitude	16 Daily	18 Daily
PM	PM		*Continued from table 4*		AM	AM
6.03	10.35	1773	Lv **Avery** (P.T.)‖I	2492	1.20	11.15
			(Idaho Div.)			
		1778	Lv Ethelton▲	2426		
		1786	Lv Marble Creek▲	2318		
		1787	Lv Pocono▲	2304		
		1795	Lv Calder▲	2195		
			St. Joe River			
f644		1806	Lv **St. Joe**	2150		f10.08
f701		1813	Lv Omera▲	2145		
7.25		1818	Lv **St. Maries** I	2145		9.48
			St. Joe River			
		1824	Lv Ramsdell▲ O	2145		
		1830	Lv Pedee▲	2315		
			Lake Chatcolet			
			Coeur d'Alene Indian Reservation			
f 8.01		1837	Lv **Plummer Jct.**▲	2653		f910
f 8.11		1843	Lv Worley▲	2642		f858
		1849	Lv Setters, Idaho▲	2582		
		1856	Lv Manito, Wash.▲	2585		
		1873	Lv Dishman▲	1990		
9.15	1.45	1879	Ar} **SPOKANE** I	1902	10.15	8.00
9.40	1.55		Lv} Spokane Falls		9.55	7.30
			Spokane River			
10.15		1896	Lv **Cheney**	2326		6.50
			Eastern Washington College of Education			
11.13		1941	Lv **Marengo**▲	1649		5.55
f11.27		1950	Lv **Ralston**▲	1667		f 5.33
11.45		1965	Lv **Lind**	1415		5.13
f12.05		1978	Lv Roxboro▲	1250		f 4.52
12.20		1988	Lv **Warden**▲	1279		4.42
12.45	4.45	2000	Ar} **Othello**‖	1039	7.27	4.27
12.55	5.00		Lv}		7.20	4.20
			(Coast Division)			
		2010	Lv Taunton▲	853		
①1.14		2015	Lv Corfu▲	743		①3.50
①1.25		2026	Lv Smyrna▲	550		①3.15
1.44		2038	Lv **Beverly**	541		
			Columbia River			
		2044	Lv Doris (Basalt Form'ns)▲	1130		
		2050	Lv Rye▲	1750		
			Johnson's Creek Tunnel, length 1,973 ft. Summit Saddle Mts. Alt. 2,455			
		2057	Lv Boylston▲	2440		
		2062	Lv Renslow▲	1975		
2.53		2067	Lv **Kittitas**▲	1545		2.08
3.11	6.57	2074	Lv **Ellensburg**	1585	5.33	1.55
			Yakima River			
⑤3.23		2080	Lv Thorp▲	1647		⑤1.42
		2089	Lv Horlick▲ O	1775		
3.58	7.31	2099	Lv **Cle Elum**‖	1935	5.01	1.15
			Yakima River			
⑤4.18		2111	Lv Easton▲	2169		⑤1258
		2119	Lv Whittier▲ O	2460		
			Lake Keechelus			
⑤4.53		2128	Lv Hyak (Ski Bowl)▲	2562		⑤1232
			Summit Cascade Mts. Snoqualmie Tunnel, length 11,888 ft.			
		2131		2564		
⑤5.00		2131	Lv Rockdale▲	2514		⑤1225
			Snoqualmie River			
		2136	Lv Bandera▲	2129		
		2141	Lv Garcia▲	1650		
		2146	Lv Ragnar▲	1195		
5.53		2150	Lv **Cedar Falls** I	938		11.40
			Cedar River			
		2155	Lv Barneston▲	790		
		2159	Lv Trude▲	636		
		2162	Lv Landsburg▲	536		
		2164	Lv Noble▲	440		
⑤6.30		2167	Lv Maple Valley▲	325		⑤1112
			Cedar River			
6.45	9.53	2177	Lv **Renton**	37	3.06	10.54
		2179	Lv **Black River**▲	27		
		2184	Lv Van Asselt▲	25		
		2185	Lv Argo▲	15		
7.30	10.30	2189	Ar} **SEATTLE**‖I	15	2.45	10.30
7.50	10.45	0	Lv} Union Station		2.30	10.00
		10	Lv **Black River**▲	37		
⑤8.20		16	Lv Kent▲	51		⑤9.20
			White River			
⑤8.28		21	Lv **Auburn**▲	81		⑤9.12
8.40		29	Lv Sumner▲	79		9.02
⑤8.44		30	Lv No. Puyallup▲	62		⑤8.58
9.05	11.45	38	Ar **Tacoma**‖I	63	1.30	8.45
AM	AM		*Milwaukee Road Station*		PM	PM
			Pacific Time			

Vertical markings for Table 5: THE COLUMBIAN, OLYMPIAN HIAWATHA, (Columbia Irrigation Area), Cascade Mountains, (Seattle Water Shed), ELECTRIFIED, (Berry and Fruit Farms).

For equipment see pages 8 to 11.

Chicago-Rockford-Dubuque-Marion (Cedar Rapids)-Des Moines-Omaha-Sioux Falls

READ DOWN   READ UP   READ DOWN   READ UP

Table 8 — Central Time

Listing of stations between Chicago and Elgin see Table 40.

SOUTHWEST LIMITED 107 Daily	THE ARROW 107 Daily	MIDWEST HIAWATHA 103 Daily	Miles	Station	MIDWEST HIAWATHA 102 Daily	THE ARROW 108 Daily	SOUTHWEST LIMITED 108 Daily
PM	PM	AM		*Union Station*	PM	AM	AM
6 10	6 10	11.50	0	Lv Chicago‖I .... Ar	8.25	8.50	8.50
⑤7.03	⑥7.03	⑪12.30	37	Lv Elgin I Lv	7.36	⑲7.50	⑩7.50
			45	Lv Pingree Grove▲ Lv			
7.22	7.22		51	Lv Hampshire Lv		7.27	7.27
			55	Lv New Lebanon▲ Lv			
f 7.32	f 7.32		59	Lv Genoa Lv		f 7.14	f 7.14
			63	Lv Kingston Lv			
f 7.41	f 7.41		68	Lv Kirkland Lv		f 7.03	f 7.03
			75	Lv Monroe Center Lv			
8.01	8.01	1.09	80	Ar Davis Jct. I Lv	6.59	6.47	6.47
8.31	8.31	1.39	12	Ar Rockford Bus Lv	6.20	6.00	6.00
6.20	6.20	12.30		Lv ...... Ar	8.31	7.17	7.17
8.01	8.01	1.09	80	Ar Davis Jct. Lv	6.59	6.47	6.47
			85	Lv Stillman Valley Lv			
				Rock River			
f 8.13	f 8.13		89	Lv Byron Lv		f 6.30	f 6.30
				Leaf River			
f 8.24	f 8.24		97	Lv Leaf River Lv		f 6.21	f 6.21
f 8.35	f 8.35		107	Lv Forreston Lv		f 6.11	f 6.11
			110	Lv Harper▲ Lv			
8.53	8.53		120	Lv Lanark Lv		5.54	5 54
9.06	9.05	1.53	128	Lv Mount Carroll Lv	⑮6.06	5.40	5.40
9.25	9.25	2.10	138	Ar Savanna I Lv	5.54	5.20	5.20
4.50	4.50		0	Lv Milwaukee‖I ..... Ar		9.45	9.45
6.56	6.56		85	Ar Beloit Lv		7.23	7.23
7.08	7.08		85	Lv		7.08	7.08
8.12	8.12		120	Ar Freeport Lv		6.10	6.10
9.05	9.05		157	Ar Savanna‖ Lv		5.10	5.10
PM							
9.50	9.55	2.18	138	Lv Savanna‖I ...... Ar	5.47	4.55	4.45
				Mississippi River			AM
			141	Lv Sabula, Ia. Lv			
⑱10.21		⑱2.35	153	Lv Green Island Lv	⑱5 27	⑨4 25	
			162	Lv Spragueville▲ Lv			
			166	Lv Prown's▲ Lv			
10.45		2.54	173	Ar Delmar Lv	5.08	3.50	
Bus-B 3.00			0	Lv Delmar .... Ar	5.00		Bus-C
Bus-A 3.20			7.6	Ar Maquoketa Lv	4.40		
4.05			41.4	Ar Dubuque Lv	3.45		
1.30			0	Lv Dubuque .... Ar	6.20		Bus-D
2.25			33.8	Ar Maquoketa Lv	5.35		
2.45			41.4	Ar Delmar Lv	5.15		
10.45		2.54	173	Lv Delmar Lv	5.08	3.50	
			180	Lv Elwood▲ Lv			
⑤10.54			185	Lv Lost Nation Lv			
11.05			192	Lv Oxford Jct. Lv		3.17	
			198	Lv Hale▲ Lv			
⑤11.16			202	Lv Olin Lv		⑦3.06	
			208	Lv Morley▲ Lv			
			214	Lv Martelle Lv			
			219	Lv Paralta▲ Lv			
11.44		3 45	227	Ar Marion‖I Lv	4.23	2.41	
④5.00			6	Ar Cedar Rapids I Bus	④3 15		
④3.15			0	Lv ..... Ar	④5.00		
11.57		3.45	227	Lv Marion‖I Lv	4.23	2.25	
⑤12.14			242	Lv Atkins Lv		⑪2.09	
			247	Lv Newhall Lv			
⑤12.27			254	Lv Van Horne Lv		⑪1.57	
⑤12.32			259	Lv Keystone Lv		⑪1.51	
			265	Lv Elberon Lv			
			269	Lv Vining▲ Lv			
1.05	4 33		281	Ar Tama Lv	3.27	1.16	
1.10	4 33		281	Ar Tama .... Ar	3.27	1.12	
			293	Lv Pickering Lv			
⑥1.26			296	Lv Ferguson Lv			
			301	Lv Haverhill Lv			
			308	Lv Melbourne Lv		⑪12.42	
			313	Lv Rhodes Lv			
⑰1.54			320	Lv Collins Lv		⑰12.30	
⑰1.59			325	Lv Maxwell Lv		⑪12.24	
⑧2.07			332	Lv Cambridge Lv			
			336	Lv Huxley Lv			
			340	Lv Slater Lv			
2.30	5 33		347	Ar Madrid Lv	2.31	12.01	
3.05	5.38		347	Lv Madrid .... Ar	2.11	11.20	
4.05	6.35		381	{ Des Moines‖I Ar	1.20	10.20	
10 20	4.25			Lv ...... Ar	3.25	4.05	
11 20	5 20		347	Ar Madrid Lv	2.34	3.05	
PM	PM			*Continued in table 9.*	PM	AM	

To Kansas City See Table 10   *From Kansas City See Table 10*

Table 9 — Central Time

For complete service between Manilla and Sioux Falls see Table 6.

THE ARROW 107 Daily	MIDWEST HIAWATHA 103 Daily	Miles	Station	MIDWEST HIAWATHA 102 Daily	THE ARROW 108 Daily
AM	PM		*Continued from table 8.*	PM	PM
2.55	5 33	347	Lv Madrid .... Ar	2 31	11 42
... ③		352	Lv Woodward Lv		③
		357	Lv Bouton Lv		
3.24	5.53	362	Lv Perry I Lv	2.08	11.20
			Raccoon River		
		368	Lv Dawson Lv		
		372	Lv Jamaica Lv		
⑫3.38		374	Lv Herndon Lv		f 10.56
		379	Lv Bagley Lv		⑲1043
⑫3.52		385	Lv Bayard Lv		10.36
4.05		392	Lv Coon Rapids Lv		
⑫4.17		400	Lv Dedham Lv		⑭10.19
		406	Lv Templeton Lv		10.09
4.35		412	Lv Manning Lv		
		417	Lv Aspinwall Lv		
5.00	6.43	423	Ar Manilla Lv	1.14	9.50
5.30	6.59	423	Lv Manilla‖ .... Ar	12.50	9.20
8.00	9.08	514	Ar Sioux City‖ Lv	10.55	6.45
8.15	9.18	514	Lv .... Ar	10.50	6.30
9.12	f 9.57	545	Lv Akron Lv	f 10.00	5.35
9.40	10.14	558	Lv Hawarden Lv	9.40	5.12
1018	10.46	583	Lv Canton Lv	9.10	4.35
1055	11.25	604	Ar Sioux Falls‖ Lv	8.40	4.00
5.30	6 56	423	Lv Manilla‖ .... Ar	1.03	9.20
5.42		431	Lv Defiance Lv		f 8.58
5.52		436	Lv Earling Lv		f 8.52
6.01		441	Lv Panama Lv		f 8.45
6.09		447	Lv Portsmouth Lv		f 8.37
6.17		453	Lv Persia Lv		f 8.30
6.35		463	Lv Neola Lv		8.19
6.53	7.56	484	Lv Council Bluffs I ... Lv	12.09	7.56
7.00		485	Lv Union Pacific Tfr., Ia.▲ .. Lv		
7.30	8.20	488	Ar Omaha, Neb.‖I ... Lv	11.55	7.40
AM	PM		*Union Station*	AM	PM

For complete service between Manilla and Sioux Falls see Table 6.

CEDAR RAPIDS CITY LINES, INC. Bus Fare—15c each way.

NOTE: Direct bus connection at Marion with MIDWEST HIAWATHA. Leave Cedar Rapids MILWAUKEE ROAD STATION 3:15 p.m. direct to Marion Station. Returning leave Marion 4:25 p.m.

Explanation of Reference Marks for Tables 8 and 9.

* Daily. † Except Sunday. § Sunday only. ‖ Meals. ▲ Non-agency station. I U. S. Mail box at station or on platform.

f Stops on signal to take or leave passengers.

① Stops to take revenue passengers for Savanna and beyond.
③ Passengers from or to Woodward will use Second District trains at South Woodward to or from Madrid where connection is made with main line trains. See table 31.
④ Direct connections at Marion for and from Cedar Rapids with buses of the Cedar Rapids City Lines. Does not carry checked baggage or dogs.
⑤ Stops to leave revenue passengers from Savanna or beyond or take revenue passengers for Marion or beyond.
⑥ Stops to take passengers.
⑦ Stops to leave revenue passengers from Madrid or beyond or take revenue passengers for Savanna or beyond.
⑧ Stops to leave revenue passengers from Savanna and beyond or take revenue passengers for beyond Madrid.
⑨ Stops to let off passengers or take passengers for Savanna or beyond.
⑩ Stops to leave revenue passengers from Hampshire, also Savanna or beyond.
⑪ Stops to take revenue passengers for beyond Green Island or leave revenue passengers from beyond Madrid.
⑫ Stops to leave revenue passengers from beyond Madrid or take revenue passengers for beyond Manilla.
⑬ Stops to leave revenue passengers from Chicago and Rockford or take revenue passengers for Dubuque, Marion or beyond.
⑭ Stops to leave revenue passengers from beyond Manilla or take revenue passengers for beyond Madrid.
⑮ Stops to leave revenue passengers from Dubuque, Marion or beyond or take revenue passengers for Chicago.
⑰ Stops to leave or take revenue passengers from or beyond Marion and for or from beyond Madrid.
⑱ Stops to leave or take revenue passengers from or for Davis Jct. or beyond or stops to take or leave revenue passengers for or from Marion or beyond.
⑲ Stops to leave revenue passengers from Manilla or beyond or take revenue passengers for Madrid or beyond.

For equipment see pages 8 to 11.

Chicago to Milwaukee
Northbound

READ DOWN

Miles	Table **19** Central Time	55 Daily AM	27 Ex. Sun. AM	29 Sun. Only AM	5 Daily AM	101 Daily PM	15 Daily PM	23 Daily PM	7 Daily PM	9 Daily PM	51 Sun. Only PM	17 Daily PM	1 Daily PM
	Union Station												
0	Lv **Chicago** ‖	1.30	8.45	9.20	10.30	1.00	3.30	3.35	6.20	7.45	9.25	10.00	11.15
3	Lv Western Ave.....												
24	Lv Deerfield........		㉖9.13			③1.23			⑲8.11			⑱10.30 ③11.45	
32	Lv **Rondout**......												
37	Lv Wilson▲.......												
39	Lv Gurnee......												
43	Lv Wadsworth.....												
47	Lv Russell, Ill.....												
52	Lv Ranney, Wis.▲	Coaches	80 Minute Train Cafe-Parlor Car-Coaches	80 Minute Train Coaches	MORNING HIAWATHA 75 Minute Train Parlor Car-Dining Car-Coaches	AFTERNOON HIAWATHA 75 Minute Train Does not carry checked baggage or dogs Parlor Car-Dining Car-Coaches	THE OLYMPIAN HIAWATHA 75 Minute Train Does not carry Coach passengers	85 Minute Train Parlor Car-Coaches Buffet Service	80 Minute Train Parlor Car-Dining Car Coaches	85 Minute Train Coaches	80 Minute Train Coaches	Coaches	Buffet Service-Coaches
53	Lv Truesdell.....												
58	Lv Somers.....												
62	Lv **Sturtevant**....								4.34				
66	Lv Franksville.....												
69	Lv Caledonia.....												
73	Lv Oakwood▲......												
78	Lv Lake......												
85	Ar **Milwaukee** ‖ ..	3.05 AM	10.05 AM	10.40 AM	11.45 AM	2.15 PM	4.45 PM	5.00 PM	7.40 PM	9.10 PM	10.45 PM	11.30 PM	12.45 AM
	Union Station												

For Suburban Service see Suburban Leaflets.
For listing of Suburban Stations see Tables 40-41.

Milwaukee to Chicago
Southbound

READ DOWN

Miles	Table **20** Central Time	56 Daily AM	4 Daily AM	18 Daily AM	24 Daily AM	12 Daily AM	16 Daily PM	6 Daily PM	46 Daily PM	100 Daily PM	14 Daily PM	58 Daily PM
	Union Station											
0	Lv **Milwaukee** ‖ ...	4.35	6.10	7.05	7.45	9.45	12.25	1.25	4.00	6.00	8.10	9.00
7	Lv Lake.........											
12	Lv Oakwood▲.....											
16	Lv Caledonia.....											
19	Lv Franksville.....											
23	Lv **Sturtevant**....											
27	Lv Somers......											
32	Lv Truesdell......	Coaches	Parlor Car Service Dining Service-Coaches	Dining Car-Coaches	THE TRAVELER 80 Minute Train Parlor Car (Ex. Sun.) Dining Car (Ex. Sun.)-Coaches	80 Minute Train Parlor Car (Ex. Sun.)-Coaches	THE OLYMPIAN HIAWATHA 80 Minute Train Seats Reserved	MORNING HIAWATHA 75 Minute Train Parlor Car-Dining Car-Coaches	80 Minute Train Parlor Car-Coaches	AFTERNOON HIAWATHA 75 Minute Train Does not carry checked baggage or dogs Parlor Car-Dining Car-Coaches	CHIPPEWA-HIAWATHA Cafe-Parlor Car-Coaches	Coaches
33	Lv Ranney, Wis.▲.											
38	Lv Russell, Ill.....											
42	Lv Wadsworth.....											
46	Lv Gurnee.......											
48	Lv Wilson▲......											
53	Lv **Rondout**.....											
61	Lv Deerfield......		⑤5.37	③7.10	⑱8.10	⑲10.08					⑱9.04	
82	Lv Western Ave.....	6.12										⑥10.20
85	Ar **Chicago** ‖	6.20 AM	8.00 AM	8.45 AM	9.05 AM	11.05 AM	1.45 PM	2.40 PM	5.20 PM	7.15 PM	9.40 PM	10.30 PM
	Union Station											

Next time try the

For equipment see pages 8 to 11.

Chicago-Milwaukee-Sault Ste. Marie

READ DOWN			READ UP
9-8 Daily PM	Miles	Table **21** Central Time	7-2-56 Daily AM
		Union Station	
7.45	0	Lv **Chicago** ‖ ....Ar	6.20
	3	Lv Western Ave..........Lv	
⑱8.11	24	Lv Deerfield...........Lv	⑤5.37
9.10	85	Ar **Milwaukee** ‖ {Lv	4.35
9.25		{Ar	4.10
10.39	139	Lv **Plymouth**........Lv	2.50
11.15	163	Lv Chilton..........Lv	2.16
	170	Lv Hilbert...........Lv	
⑤1158	192	Lv DePere..........Lv	
12.10	197	Ar **Green Bay** (Washington St.) {Lv	1.05
12.25		{Ar	12.50
f 1.10	213	Lv Sobieski.........Lv	f12.25
f 1.16	217	Lv Abrams.........Lv	f12.20
f 1.24	224	Lv Stiles Jct........Lv	
1.30	229	Lv Lena..........Lv	
1.41	237	Lv Coleman.........Lv	11.55
f 1.45	239	Lv Pound..........Lv	
	243	Lv Beaver▲........Lv	
2.02	248	Lv Crivitz..........Lv	11.37
	253	Lv Middle Inlet▲.....Lv	
f 2.18	259	Lv Wausaukee.......Lv	f11.20
	268	Lv Amberg.........Lv	
3.05	278	Ar **Pembine** (Milw. Road)..Lv	10.20
5.22	278	Lv **Pembine** (Soo Line)...Ar	10.10
f 5.43	291	Lv Faithorn.........Lv	9.44
5.58	299	Lv Hermansville......Lv	9.29
6.45	331	Ar Gladstone........Lv	8.35
⑪		Ar } Bus..Escanaba..Bus { Ar⑪	
⑪		Lv } { Lv⑪	
7.00	331	Lv Gladstone........Lv	8.20
7.33	350	Lv Nahma Jct........Lv	7.47
8.15	375	Lv **Manistique**......Lv	7.10
8.34	386	Lv Gulliver.........Lv	6.44
9.05	404	Lv Gould City.......Lv	6.19
9.17	410	Lv Engadine........Lv	6.09
10.04	438	Ar **Trout Lake**......Ar	5.03
11.05	458	Lv Rudyard.........Lv	4.31
★1145	482	Ar **Sault Ste. Marie**...Lv	3.50
AM		*Soo Line Station*	PM

For complete schedules between Chicago and Pembine, see Table 22.

Explanation of
Reference Marks for Tables 19 to 24, Inclusive

* Daily.   † Except Sunday.   § Sunday only.
‖ Meals.   ▲ Non-agency station.
f Stops on signal to take or leave passengers.
★ Local time observed is 1 hour earlier than shown in timetable.
① Stops to leave revenue passengers from Wausau or beyond.
② Connection by bus to and from Coleman. See table 43.
③ Stops to take revenue passengers for New Lisbon and beyond.
④ Stops to leave revenue passengers from St. Paul or beyond.
⑤ Stops to leave passengers from Milwaukee or beyond.
⑥ Stops Sundays to leave revenue passengers.
⑦ Stops to leave revenue passengers from beyond Milwaukee.
⑧ Stops to leave from or take for Milwaukee or beyond or take for or leave from Green Bay or beyond.
⑨ Stops to leave revenue passengers from beyond New Lisbon or take revenue passengers for Wausau or beyond.
⑩ Stops to take revenue passengers for Green Bay or beyond.
⑪ Connecting bus service between Gladstone and Escanaba.
⑫ Stops to take revenue passengers for beyond Milwaukee.
⑬ Stops to leave or take passengers from or for Milwaukee or beyond.
⑭ Connection made by Bus from Portage.
⑮ Stops to leave revenue passengers from beyond New Lisbon or take revenue passengers for Milwaukee or beyond.
⑯ Stops to take revenue passengers for beyond New Lisbon.
⑰ Stops to leave revenue passengers from north of New Lisbon.
⑱ Stops to leave passengers from Milwaukee or beyond.
⑲ Stops on signal to take passengers from No. 26.
⑳ Stops to take revenue passengers for Milwaukee or beyond.
㉒ Stops to leave passengers from New Lisbon or beyond.
㉔ Will wait 30 minutes for passengers from No. 9, The Copper Country Limited.

Light numerals indicate a.m. **Dark numerals indicate p.m.**

Chicago-Green Bay-Ontonagon-Houghton-Calumet

READ DOWN / READ UP

THE COPPER COUNTRY LIMITED	CHIPPEWA-HIAWATHA	Miles	Table 22 Central Time	THE COPPER COUNTRY LIMITED	CHIPPEWA-HIAWATHA
9 Daily	101 21 Daily			2-56 Daily	14 Daily
PM	PM		*Union Station*	AM	PM
7.45	■1.00	0	Lv Chicago ‖ .... Ar	6.20	9.40
		3	Lv Western Ave. Lv		
⑨8.11	1.23	24	Lv Deerfield Lv	⑦5.37	⑱9.04
		62	Lv Sturtevant Lv		
9.10	2.15	85	Ar Milwaukee ‖ { Lv	4.35	8.10
9.25	2.25		Lv ‖ { Ar	4.10	7.50
		93	Lv No. Milwaukee ... Lv		
		98	Lv Brown Deer▲ Lv		
		102	Lv Thiensville Lv		
		107	Lv Cedarburg Lv		
		109	Lv Grafton Lv		
		113	Lv Saukville Lv		
	⑧3.08	120	Lv Fredonia Lv		⑧6.54
		125	Lv Random Lake Lv		⑧6.47
10.20		130	Lv Adell Lv	⑧3.01	
10.25		134	Lv Waldo Lv		
10.39	3.32	139	Lv Plymouth Lv	2.50	6.30
10.55	⑧3.45	146	Lv Elkhart Lake Lv	⑧2.38	⑧6.14
⑧11.01	⑧3.52	152	Lv Kiel Lv		⑧6.05
11.07		156	Lv New Holstein Lv		⑧6.00
11.15	4.05	163	Lv Chilton Lv	2.16	5.51
	⑧4.15	170	Lv Hilbert Lv		⑧5.41
		175	Lv Forest Jct. Lv		
		183	Lv Greenleaf Lv		
11.53	⑧4.42	192	Lv De Pere Lv		⑧5.13
12.25	4.50	196	Ar Green Bay { Lv	1.25	5.05
12.25	4.58		Lv Washington St. { Ar	1.15	4.58
12.50	5.05	198	Ar Green Bay { Lv	1.05	4.50
12.50	5.22		Lv Oakland Ave. { Ar	12.50	4.35
1.10		213	Lv Sobieski Lv	f 12.25	
1.16		217	Lv Abrams Lv	f 12.20	
1.24	f 5 57	224	Lv Stiles Jct. Lv		4.01
1.30		229	Lv Lena Lv		f 3.55
1.41	6.14	237	Ar Coleman Lv	11.55	3.45
	6.15		Lv Coleman .... Ar		3.35
	6.59		Ar Marinette Lv		2.55
	7.04		Ar Menominee Lv		2.50
	2.30		Lv Menominee ...... Ar		7.04
	2.55		Lv Marinette Lv		6.59
	3.35		Ar Coleman Lv		6.15
1.41	6.14	237	Lv Coleman Lv	11.55	3 45
1.45	②	239	Lv Pound Lv		②
		242	Lv Beaver▲ Lv		
2.02	6.31	248	Lv Crivitz Lv	11 37	3.29
		253	Lv Middle Inlet▲ Lv		
2.18	6.46	259	Lv Wausaukee Lv	f 11.20	3 13
	f 6 58	268	Lv Amberg Lv		f 2 58
3.05	7.14	278	Lv Pembine, Wis. ... Lv	10.50	2 43
3.45	7.32	291	Lv Iron Mt., Mich. ... Lv	10.00	2.25
		305	Lv Randville▲ Lv	f 9 30	
4.20	8.02	312	Lv Sagola Lv	§ 9 21	1 48
4.55	8.30	315	Ar Channing ‖ Lv	9.15	1 40
		323	Lv Kelso Jct.▲ Lv		
		335	Lv Amasa Lv	12 35	
	9 01	348	Lv Park Siding▲ Lv	f 12 15	
	f 9 20	362	Lv Sidnaw Lv	11 52	
	9.45	381	Lv Pori▲ Lv	f 11.20	
	f 10.16	383	Lv Rousseau▲ Lv		
		388	Lv McKeever▲ Lv		
	10.30	389	Lv Mass Lv	11.04	
	10.45	396	Lv Rockland▲ Lv	f 10 48	
	11.10	408	Ar Ontonagon Lv	10.25	
4.55	PM	315	Lv Channing ‖ ...... Ar	9 03	AM
5.18		327	Lv Witch Lake▲ Lv	f 8 51	
5.22		330	Lv Witbeck▲ Lv	f 8 5.	
5.35		337	Lv Republic Lv	8 23	
6.00		347	Ar Champion { Lv	8 00	
6.10			Lv D.S.S. & A. { Ar	7.53	
6.21		353	Lv Michigamme Lv	7.48	
6.37		358	Lv Nestoria Lv	7.2.	
7.08		378	Lv L'Anse Lv	6.53	
7.27		384	Lv Baraga Lv	6.44	
		385	Lv Keweenaw Bay▲ .. Lv		
★8.10		410	Lv Houghton Lv	★6 03	
★8.20		411	Lv Hancock Lv	★5 43	
8.55		424	Ar Calumet Lv	★5.15	
AM			*D.S.S. & A. Station*	PM	

For equipment see pages 8 to 11.

Chicago-Wisconsin Rapids-Wausau-Minocqua

READ DOWN / READ UP

THE TOMAHAWK	HIAWATHA North Woods Service	Miles	Table 23 Central Time	HIAWATHA North Woods Service	THE TOMAHAWK	THE TOMAHAWK	
1-217 Daily	101-201 Daily			200-100 Daily	256-56 Ex. Sun.	202-56 Sun. Only	58-14 Daily
PM	PM		*Union Station*	PM	AM	AM	PM
11.15	❡1.00	0	Lv Chicago ‖ .... Ar	7.15	6.20	6.20	9.40
		3	Lv Western Ave. Lv		6.12	6.12	
③11.45	⑫1.23	24	Lv Deerfield Lv		⑦5.37	⑦5.37	⑱9.04
		62	Lv Sturtevant Lv				
12.45	2.15	85	Ar Milwaukee ‖ { Lv	6 00	4.35	4.35	8.10
12.55	2.15		{ Ar	5.55	4.22	4.22	7.43
		118	Lv Oconomowoc Lv				6.55
1.30		131	Lv Watertown Lv	5.10	3.22	3.22	6.30
		150	Lv Columbus Lv		⑰2.54	⑰2.54	5.59
2.27	3.32	178	Ar Portage ‖ Lv	4 32	2.24	2.24	5.15
10.30	2.00	0	Lv Madison .... Ar	6 00	8.05	8.05	
11.45	3.15	37	Ar Portage ‖ Lv	4.40	6.40	7.10	
2.37	3.34	178	Lv Portage ‖ .... Ar	4 30	2.14	2.14	5 05
2.54	⑭	195	Lv Wisconsin Dells ... Lv	⑱1.55	1.55		4 43
3.34	4.11	221	Ar New Lisbon ‖ { Lv	3 57	1.28	1.28	4 05
4.15	4.15		{ Lv	3 35	12.20	12.20	PM
4.33	⑨4.30	233	Lv Necedah Lv	3.10	12.01	12.01	
		247	Lv Finley▲ Lv				
5.07	⑧5.00	254	Lv Babcock Lv	2 40	11.27	11.27	
5.31		267	Lv Nekoosa Lv		11.00		
5.43	5.18	270	Lv Port Edwards Lv	2 23	10 48	10 53	
6.10	5.30	274	Lv Wisc. Rapids Lv	2.15	10 40	10 45	
6.24		281	Lv Rudolph Lv		10.21	10.28	
6.38	5.55	287	Lv Junction City Lv	1.48	10.07	10.19	
6.50		296	Lv Dancy▲ Lv		9.57	10.08	
			Wisconsin River				
6.55		298	Lv Knowlton Lv		9.51	10 03	
7.10	6.20	304	Lv Mosinee Lv	1.25	9.42	9.55	
7.25	㉒6.30	311	Lv Rothschild Lv	1.14	9.29	9.42	
			Eau Claire River				
7.30		313	Lv Schofield Lv		9.24	9 38	
8.00	6.50	317	Lv Wausau Lv	1 01	9.15	9.30	
8.13		322	Lv Brokaw Lv	f 12.42	8.40	9.13	
			Prairie River				
8.43	7.25	336	Lv Merrill ‖ Lv	12.15	8.10	8.53	
f 9.10	①7.46	349	Lv Irma▲ Lv	11.58	f 7.46	f 8.34	
			Wisconsin River				
9.29	8.02	358	Lv Tomahawk Lv	11.44	7.29	8 21	
9.43	8.10	364	Lv Heafford Jct. Lv	f 11.33	7.15	8.10	
10.00	①8.24	373	Lv Harshaw Lv	f 11.19	7.00	7 54	
f 10.03	①8.33	375	Lv Goodnow▲ Lv		f 6 52	f 7 45	
10.25	f 8.47	384	Lv Hazelhurst▲ Lv	10.59	6.39	7 31	
f 10.30	①8.51	386	Lv Rantz▲ Lv		f 6 36	f 7 23	
	①8.54	388	Lv Kawaga▲ Lv		f 6 33	f 7 23	
10.40	9.00	389	Ar Minocqua Lv	10.50		7.20	7 20
10.50		391	Ar Woodruff Lv	10.40			
AM	PM			AM	PM	PM	

❡ Does not carry checked baggage or dogs between Chicago-Madison and New Lisbon. No baggage handled between New Lisbon and Minocqua Sunday only.
■ Does not carry checked baggage from Chicago to Milwaukee.

Chicago-Crystal Falls-Iron River

READ DOWN / READ UP

9 Daily	101-21 Daily	Miles	Table 24 Central Time	14 Daily	2-56 Daily
PM	PM		*Union Station*	PM	AM
7.45	■1.00	0	Lv Chicago ‖ .... Ar	9.40	6 20
⑲8.11	⑫1.23	24	Lv Deerfield Lv	⑱9.04	⑦5.37
		62	Lv Sturtevant Lv		
	2.25	85	Ar Milwaukee ‖ Lv	7.50	4.10
10.39	3.32	139	Lv Plymouth Lv	6.30	2.50
	4.15	170	Lv Hilbert Lv	⑧5.41	
11.53	4.42	192	Lv De Pere Lv	⑧5.13	
12.10	4.50	197	Ar Green Bay { Lv	5.05	1.25
12.25	4.58		Lv Washington St. { Ar	4.53	1.15
1.41	6.14	237	Lv Coleman Lv	3.45	11 53
2.02	6.31	248	Lv Crivitz Lv	3.29	11 55
2.18	6.46	259	Lv Wausaukee Lv	3.13	f 11 .0
3.05	7.14	278	Lv Pembine Lv	2.45	10 5.
3.45	7.32	291	Lv Iron Mountain ... Lv	2.25	10.00
4.20	8.02	312	Lv Sagola Lv	1.4.	1.40
4.30		315	Ar Channing ‖ { Lv	9 15	
5.15	8.15		Lv { Ar	PM	8.05
		323	Lv Kelso Jct.▲ Lv		
5.55	8.38	330	Lv Crystal Falls Lv	1 10	7.23
6.00	8.40	333	Lv Fortune Lake▲ ... Lv	f 12 55	f 7 13
6.40		349	Lv Stambaugh Lv	12 30	6.57
6.50	9.10	350	Ar Iron River Lv	12.25	6.50

Bus columns: Bus F Daily, Bus D Daily, Bus C Daily, Bus A Daily, Bus B Daily, Bus E Daily

Bus F: f 5.25 AM — Bus D: f 4.20 / 4.30 PM, 8.20 / 8.15 PM/AM — Bus C: 8.02 / 8.10 / 1.50 PM — Bus A: 1.40 PM / 9.15 PM — Bus B: f 7.53 PM / 8.05 — Bus E: 4.34 / 4.45 AM

8

Cancel Reservations Promptly if Your Plans are Changed

EQUIPMENT—WEST AND NORTHBOUND

No. 1—THE PIONEER LIMITED (See Table 1)

Union Station	Daily
Lv Chicago	11.15PM
Lv Milwaukee	12.55AM
Lv Oconomowoc	1.30AM
Lv Portage	2.37AM
Lv New Lisbon	3.34AM
Lv Tomah	4.00AM
Lv Sparta	4.35AM
Ar La Crosse	5.15AM
Ar St. Paul	8.00AM
Ar Minneapolis	8.40AM

Pullman Standard Sleeping Cars
Chicago to St. Paul-Minneapolis
8 Duplex Roomette, 6 Roomette, 4 Double Bedrooms [14-15-16]
16 Duplex Roomette, 4 Double Bedrooms [11-12]
△Milwaukee to St. Paul-Minneapolis
8 Duplex Roomette, 6 Roomette, 4 Double Bedrooms [17]

Tip Top Tap Diner
Chicago to St. Paul-Minneapolis
*Buffet Service and Beverages
A la carte or club breakfast*

Reclining Seat Lounge Coaches
Chicago to St. Paul-Minneapolis

Note: *Sleeping Cars ready for occupancy in Chicago, at 9.30 p.m. Coaches 10.30 p.m.*

Nos. 1-217—THE TOMAHAWK (See Table 23)

Union Station	Daily
Lv Chicago (No. 1)	11.15PM
Lv Milwaukee	12.55AM
Lv Portage	2.37AM
Lv New Lisbon (No. 217)	4.15AM
Ar Wisconsin Rapids	6.00AM
Ar Junction City	6.38AM
Ar Mosinee	7.10AM
Ar Wausau	7.50AM
Ar Merrill	8.40AM
Ar Tomahawk	9.27AM
Ar Minocqua	10.40AM
Ar Woodruff	10.50AM

Standard Sleeping Cars
Chicago to Minocqua
10 Sections-Compartments-Drawing Room [18]
△Milwaukee to Minocqua-Woodruff
15 Sections-Compartments-Drawing Room [19] *Ex. Sat.*

Reclining Seat Lounge Coach
Chicago to Minocqua-Woodruff

Note: *Sleeping Cars ready for occupancy in Chicago at 9.30 p.m. Coaches, 10.30 p.m.*

No. 11-103—Chicago to Austin (See Tables 7 and 12)

Union Station	Daily
Lv Chicago (No. 11)	9.30PM
Ar Walworth	10.53PM
Ar Janesville	11.28PM
Ar Madison	12.30AM
Ar Calmar	5.20AM
Ar Austin (No. 103)	7.35AM

⊙**Pullman Sleeping Car**
Chicago to Austin
8 Sections-2 Comp't-Drawing Room [112] *(Ex. Sat.)*

Reclining Seat Lounge Coach
Chicago to Calmar
Calmar to Austin

No. 5—THE MORNING HIAWATHA (See Table 1)

Union Station	Daily
Lv Chicago	10.30AM
Lv Milwaukee	11.52AM
Lv Oconomowoc	12.28PM
Lv Watertown	12.44PM
Lv Portage	1.33PM
Ar Wisconsin Dells	1.50PM
Ar Sparta	2.55PM
Ar La Crosse	3.27PM
Ar Winona	4.02PM
Ar Red Wing	5.13PM
Ar Hastings	5.35PM
Ar St. Paul	6.05PM
Ar Minneapolis	6.45PM

Skytop Lounge Drawing Room Parlor Car
Chicago to St. Paul-Minneapolis [P-50]

Dining Car
Chicago to St. Paul-Minneapolis
Club breakfast; table d'hote luncheon and dinner. Also a la carte service

Tip Top Tap Car-Radio
Chicago to St. Paul-Minneapolis
Buffet Service and Beverages

Reclining Seat Lounge Coaches
Chicago to St. Paul-Minneapolis

No. 5—Minneapolis to Aberdeen (See Table 2)

Milwaukee Road Station	Daily
Lv Minneapolis	8.30PM
Lv Montevideo	1.00AM
Lv Ortonville	2.12AM
Ar Aberdeen	6.10AM

Coaches
Minneapolis to Aberdeen

No. 7-111—Chicago-Milwaukee-Madison (See Table 15)

Union Station	Daily
Lv Chicago (No. 7)	6.20PM
Lv Milwaukee (No. 111)	7.55PM
Lv Oconomowoc	8.33PM
Lv Watertown	8.48PM
Ar Franklin St.	9.35PM
Ar Madison	9.40PM

Drawing Room Parlor Car
Chicago to Madison [P-70]

Dining Car
Chicago to Milwaukee
Table d'hote or a la carte dinner

Reclining Seat Lounge Coaches
Chicago to Madison

No. 9-8—THE COPPER COUNTRY LIMITED (See Tables 21 and 22)

Union Station	Daily
Lv Chicago (Milw. Road No. 9)	7.45PM
Lv Milwaukee	9.25PM
Ar Green Bay	12.10AM
Ar Crivitz	2.02AM
Ar Wausaukee	2.18AM
Ar Pembine	3.05AM
Lv Pembine (Soo Line No. 8)	5.22AM
Ar Gladstone (Escanaba)	6.45AM
Ar Sault Ste. Marie	11.45AM
Ar Iron Mountain (No. 9)	3.30AM
Ar Crystal Falls (Bus)	5.55AM
Ar Iron River	6.50AM
Ar Champion	6.00AM
Lv Champion (D.S.S.&A.&M.R. No.9)	6.10AM
Ar Houghton	8.04AM
Ar Hancock	8.20AM
Ar Calumet	8.55AM

Pullman Standard Sleeping Car
Chicago to Calumet
10 Sections-Comp't-Drawing Room [90]

Standard Sleeping Cars
Chicago to Sault Ste. Marie
10 Sections-2 Compts. [92]

Dining Service
Pembine to Sault Ste. Marie

Reclining Seat Lounge Coaches
Chicago to Pembine-Calumet
Chicago to Channing

Bus
Channing to Iron River

Coaches
Pembine to Sault Ste. Marie

No. 11—THE SIOUX (See Tables 7 and 13)

Union Station	Daily
Lv Chicago	9.30PM
Ar Walworth	10.53PM
Ar Janesville	11.28PM
Ar Madison	12.30AM
Ar Charles City	7.05AM
Ar Mason City	8.00AM
Ar Canton	2.40PM
Lv Canton	2.55PM
Ar Sioux Falls (Taxi)	

Standard Sleeping Car
Chicago to Canton
10 Sec.-Comp't-Drawing Room [110]

Pullman Standard Sleeper
Chicago to Austin [112] *(Ex. Sat.)*
8 Section-2 Comp't-Drawing Room

Reclining Seat Lounge Coaches
Chicago to Canton

Note: *Passengers destined to Harrisburg and Sioux Falls will be handled by taxi from Canton. Rail tickets are honored in taxi.*

No. 15—THE OLYMPIAN HIAWATHA (See Tables 1 to 5)

Union Station	Example	Daily
Lv Chicago (Central Time)	Sun.	3.30PM
Lv Milwaukee	"	4.45PM
Lv LaCrosse	"	7.33PM
Lv St. Paul	"	9.45PM
Ar Minneapolis	"	10.15PM
Lv Minneapolis	"	10.25PM
Ar Aberdeen	Mon.	3.18AM
Lv Aberdeen	"	3.33AM
Ar Mobridge	"	5.05AM
Lv Mobridge (Mountain Time)	"	4.10AM
Ar Miles City	"	9.30AM
Ar Harlowton	"	1.05PM
Ar Three Forks	"	3.57PM
Lv Three Forks	"	5.48PM
Ar Butte	"	6.40PM
Ar Deer Lodge	"	8.18PM
Ar Missoula	"	10.35PM
Lv Avery (Pacific Time)	"	1.45AM
Ar Spokane	Tue.	10.30AM
Ar Seattle		11.45AM
Ar Tacoma		

Pullman Skytop Lounge-Sleeping Car
Chicago to Seattle-Tacoma
8 Double Bedrooms [152]

Pullman Bedroom Car
Chicago to Seattle-Tacoma
10 Roomettes-6 Double Bedrooms [151]

Touralux Sleeping Cars
Chicago to Seattle-Tacoma
14 Sections [A-15 B-15]

Drawing Room Parlor Car
Chicago to St. Paul-Minneapolis [P-150]

Dining Car
Chicago to Seattle-Tacoma
Table d'hote luncheon and dinner. Club breakfast. Also a la carte service.

Tip-Top Grill Car
Chicago to Seattle-Tacoma
Buffet Service and Beverages.

Reclining Seat Lounge Coaches
Chicago to Seattle-Tacoma
Reserved Seats

TICKETS—The following classes of transportation will not be honored: Clergy, Charity, Employee, D.V.S., V.A.H., Blind and Attendant, Circus, Banana Messenger, Drover's, Caretaker tickets and Livestock Contracts.

No. 17—THE COLUMBIAN (See Tables 1 to 5)

Union Station	Example	Daily
Lv Chicago (Central Time)	Sun.	10.00PM
Lv Milwaukee	"	11.40PM
Ar La Crosse	Mon.	3.45AM
Ar Winona	"	4.27AM
Ar St. Paul	"	6.55AM
Lv St. Paul	"	7.15AM
Ar Minneapolis	"	7.40AM
Lv Minneapolis	"	7.55AM
Lv Montevideo	"	11.00AM
Lv Aberdeen	"	2.30PM
Ar Mobridge	"	3.15PM
Lv Mobridge (Mountain Time)	"	3.45PM
Ar Harlowton	Tues.	5.45AM
Ar Three Forks	"	9.08AM
Lv Three Forks	"	9.18AM
Ar Butte	"	11.44AM
Ar Deer Lodge	"	12.50PM
Ar Missoula	"	2.50PM
Ar Avery	"	6.53PM
Lv Avery (Pacific Time)	"	6.03PM
Ar St. Maries	"	7.25PM
Ar Spokane	"	9.15PM
Ar Seattle	Wed.	7.30AM
Ar Tacoma		9.05AM

Pullman Standard Sleeping Cars
Chicago to Seattle-Tacoma
6 Sections, 6 Double Bedrooms [171]
Chicago to St. Paul-Minneapolis
10Sec.,1Drawing Rm. 1 Comp't [176]
△Spokane to Seattle-Tacoma
10 Sec.-Buffet-Lounge [178]

Tourist Sleeping Cars
Chicago to Seattle-Tacoma
14 Sections [K-17]

Diner-Lounge Car
Chicago to Seattle-Tacoma
Club breakfast; table d'hote luncheon and dinner. Also a la carte service

Reclining Seat Lounge Coaches
Chicago to Seattle-Tacoma

Note: *Sleeping Cars ready for occupancy in Chicago at 9.00 p.m. Coaches, 9.15 p.m.*

▲May be occupied until 7.30 a.m. ⊙May be occupied until 8.00 a.m. ☐Ready for occupancy at 9.30 p.m. △Ready for occupancy at 9.00 p.m.

NOTE: Appendix C equipment listings match schedules and trains in Appendix B.

EQUIPMENT—WEST AND NORTHBOUND

No. 101-21—THE CHIPPEWA-HIAWATHA   (See Table 22 and 24)

TWIN CITIES HIAWATHA
Chicago to Milwaukee

Lv Chicago, *Union Station* .... Daily	1.00 PM
Lv Milwaukee....................	2.25 PM
Ar Green Bay....................	4.50 PM
Ar Coleman......................	6.14 PM
Ar Marinette....(Bus)...........	6.59 PM
Ar Menominee....(Bus)..........	7.04 PM
Ar Crivitz......................	6.31 PM
Ar Wausaukee...................	6.46 PM
Ar Iron Mountain...............	7.32 PM
Ar Channing....................	8.10 PM
Lv Channing....................	8.30 PM
Ar Sidnaw......................	9.45 PM
Ar Ontonagon..................	11.10 PM

Skytop Lounge Parlor Car
Chicago to Milwaukee [1010]

Cafe Parlor Car
Milwaukee to Channing [210]

Dining-Buffet Service
Chicago to Milwaukee-Channing
Table d'hote luncheon and dinner

Reclining Seat Lounge Coaches
Chicago to Milwaukee
Milwaukee to Channing-Ontonagon

Note: *Does not carry checked baggage or dogs Chicago to Milwaukee.*

No. 23 and 23-27—Chicago-Milwaukee-Madison   (See Table 15)

Union Station	Ex. Sun.		Sun. Only
Lv Chicago.....	3.35 PM	No. 23 ... 3.35 PM	
Ar Milwaukee ..	5.00 PM		5.00 PM
Lv Milwaukee...	5.15 PM	No. 27.. 5.15 PM	
Lv Oconomowoc	6.21 PM	....	5.53 PM
Lv Watertown..	6.42 PM	....	6.07 PM
Ar Franklin St..	7.31 PM	....	6.44 PM
Ar Madison.....	7.40 PM	....	6.50 PM

Parlor Car
Chicago to Madison [P-231]

Dining-Buffet Service
Chicago to Madison
Table d'hote or a la carte dinner

Reclining Seat Lounge Coaches
Chicago to Madison

No. 101-29 and 101-47—Chicago-Milwaukee-Madison   (See Table 15)

Union Station	Ex. Sat.-Sun.	Sat. Only
Lv Chicago......	1.00 PM	1.00 PM
Ar Milwaukee....	2.15 PM	2.15 PM
Lv Milwaukee....	2.18 PM	2.18 PM
Ar Oconomowoc .	2.52 PM	3.02 PM
Ar Watertown...	3.04 PM	3.15 PM
Ar Franklin St...	3.43 PM	4.02 PM
Ar Madison......	3.48 PM	4.07 PM

Parlor Cars
Chicago to Milwaukee [P-1010-P-1011]

Dining Car
Chicago to Milwaukee
Table d'hote or a la carte luncheon

Reclining Seat Lounge Coaches
Chicago to Milwaukee
Milwaukee to Madison

No. 33—ON WISCONSIN   (See Table 15)

	Ex. Sun.
Lv Milwaukee....................	7.35 AM
Lv Oconomowoc.................	8.18 AM
Lv Watertown..................	8.37 AM
Ar Franklin St.................	9.30 AM
Ar Madison.....................	9.35 AM

Reclining Seat Lounge Coaches

No. 101—THE AFTERNOON HIAWATHA   (See Table 1)

	Daily
Lv Chicago *Union Station*	1.00 PM
Lv Milwaukee....................	2.15 PM
Lv Madison.....................	2.00 PM
Lv Portage....................	3.34 PM
Ar New Lisbon.................	4.11 PM
Ar La Crosse..................	5.00 PM
Ar Winona.....................	5.34 PM
Ar Red Wing..................	6.32 PM
Ar St. Paul..................	7.15 PM
Ar Minneapolis...............	7.45 PM

Skytop Lounge Drawing Room Parlor Car
Chicago to St. Paul-Minneapolis [P-1010]

Drawing Room-Parlor Car
Chicago to St. Paul-Minneapolis [P-1011]

Dining Car
Chicago to St. Paul-Minneapolis
Table d'hote luncheon and dinner
Also a la carte service

Tip Top Tap Car-Radio
Chicago to St. Paul-Minneapolis
Buffet Service and Beverages

Reclining Seat Lounge Coaches

Note: *Does not carry checked baggage or dogs.*

No. 101-201—THE HIAWATHA—North Woods Service   (See Table 23)

Union Station	Daily
Lv Chicago....(No. 101)........	1.00 PM
Lv Milwaukee..................	2.15 PM
Lv Madison...................	2.00 PM
Lv Portage...................	3.34 PM
Ar New Lisbon...............	4.11 PM
Lv New Lisbon (No. 201)......	4.15 PM
Ar Wisconsin Rapids..........	5.30 PM
Ar Junction City.............	5.55 PM
Ar Mosinee..................	6.20 PM
Ar Wausau..................	6.50 PM
Ar Minocqua................	9.00 PM

Parlor Cars
Chicago to New Lisbon [P-1010—P-1011]

Cafe Parlor Car
New Lisbon to Minocqua [P-2010]

Dining and Buffet Service
Chicago to New Lisbon
New Lisbon to Minocqua
Table d'hote luncheon and dinner
Also a la carte service

Reclining Seat Lounge Coaches
Chicago to Portage-New Lisbon
New Lisbon to Minocqua
Madison to Portage

Note: *Does not carry checked baggage or dogs. Chicago-Madison to New Lisbon and between New Lisbon and Minocqua Sunday only.*

No. 103—THE MIDWEST HIAWATHA   (See Tables 6, 8 and 9)

Union Station	
Lv Chicago ....(Daily)....	11.50 AM
Lv Davis Jct...................	1.09 PM
Ar Rockford ....(Bus).....	1.39 PM
Lv Rockford ....(Bus).....	12.30 PM
Ar Savanna	2.10 PM
Ar Dubuque ....(Bus).....	4.05 PM
Lv Dubuque ....(Bus).....	1.30 PM
Ar Marion *(Cedar Rapids)*	3.45 PM
Ar Madrid...................	5.33 PM
Ar Des Moines .....(Bus) ...	6.35 PM
Lv Des Moines .....(Bus) ...	4.25 PM
Ar Manilla	6.43 PM
Ar Council Bluffs............	7.56 PM
Ar Omaha...................	8.20 PM
Lv Manilla ....(No. 133) ..	6.59 PM
Ar Sioux City...............	9.08 PM
Ar Canton..................	10.46 PM
Ar Sioux Falls..............	11.25 PM

Beaver-Tail Drawing Room Parlor Car
Chicago to Manilla-Sioux City-Sioux Falls [P-1030]

Tip Top Tap-Diner
Chicago to Manilla-Sioux City
Table d'hote luncheon and dinner
Also a la carte service. Buffet Service

Reclining Seat Lounge Coaches
Chicago to Council Bluffs-Omaha
Chicago to Sioux City-Sioux Falls

Bus *between*
Madrid and Des Moines
Dubuque and Delmar

Note: *Does not carry checked baggage or dogs for or from Cedar Rapids.*

No. 107—THE ARROW   (See Tables 6, 8 and 9)

Union Station	
Lv Chicago.....Daily...(No. 107)..	6.10 PM
Lv Elgin.....................	7.03 PM
Ar Davis Jct.................	8.01 PM
Ar Savanna..................	9.25 PM
Lv Milwaukee........(No. 25)..	4.50 PM
Lv Beloit...................	7.08 PM
Lv Freeport.................	8.12 PM
Ar Savanna.................	9.05 PM
Lv Savanna ....(No. 107)..	9.55 PM
Ar Marion *(Cedar Rapids)*	11.44 PM
Ar Tama....................	1.05 AM
Ar Madrid..................	2.30 AM
Ar Des Moines ....(No. 208)	4.05 AM
Lv Des Moines ....(No. 209)	10.20 PM
Lv Madrid ....(No. 107)	2.55 AM
Ar Manilla.................	5.00 AM
Lv Manilla ....(No. 217)..	5.30 AM
Ar Sioux City..............	8.00 AM
Ar Sioux Falls.............	10.55 AM
Lv Manilla ....(No. 107)..	5.30 AM
Ar Council Bluffs...........	6.53 AM
Ar Omaha..................	7.30 AM

Pullman Bedroom-Lounge Car
Chicago to Sioux City-Sioux Falls
6 Single, 2 Double Bedrooms [1070]

Pullman Standard Sleeping Cars
Chicago to Council Bluffs-Omaha
8 Sections-2 Comp't-Drawing Room [1071]
Chicago to Sioux City-Sioux Falls
12 Sections-Drawing Room [1072]

Dining-Buffet Service
Chicago to Savanna
Table d'hote or a la carte dinner
Manilla to Sioux City-Sioux Falls
Club or a la carte breakfast

Reclining Seat Lounge Coaches
Chicago to Madrid-Omaha
Chicago to Sioux City-Sioux Falls
Milwaukee to Savanna
Madrid to Des Moines

No. 107-25—THE SOUTHWEST LIMITED   (See Tables 8, 10 and 11)

Union Station	Daily
Lv Chicago...........(No. 107)..	6.10 PM
Lv Elgin...........(No. 107)..	7.03 PM
Lv Davis Jct...............	8.01 PM
Lv Milwaukee ....No. 25..	4.50 PM
Lv Delavan................	6.22 PM
Lv Beloit.................	7.08 PM
Lv Freeport..............	8.12 PM
Lv Savanna ....(No. 107)..	9.55 PM
Ar Des Moines .....(No. 208)..	4.05 AM
Ar Omaha.........(No. 107)..	7.30 AM
Ar Sioux City.....(No. 217)..	8.00 AM
Ar Sioux Falls......... " ..	10.55 AM
Lv Savanna ....(No. 25)..	9.50 PM
Lv Davenport..............	11.39 PM
Ar Ottumwa *(Sherman St.)*........	2.07 AM
Ar Excelsior Springs........	6.16 AM
Ar Kansas City.............	7.25 AM

Pullman Standard Sleeping Cars
Chicago to Kansas City
10 Sections-Drawing Room [1074]

Dining-Buffet Service
Chicago to Savanna
Table d'hote or a la carte dinner

Reclining Seat Lounge Coaches
Chicago to Savanna-Omaha
Chicago to Savanna-Sioux City-Sioux Falls
Milwaukee to Savanna-Kansas City
Savanna to Madrid-Omaha
Madrid to Des Moines

No. 117—THE VARSITY   (See Tables 15 and 16)

Lv Chicago *Union Station* ......Daily	9.30 AM
Ar Walworth...................	10.48 AM
Ar Janesville.................	11.20 AM
Ar Madison...................	12.20 PM

Cafe Parlor Car
Chicago to Madison [P-1170]
Buffet Lunch

Reclining Seat Lounge Coaches
Chicago to Madison

EQUIPMENT—EAST AND SOUTHBOUND

No. 132-102—Sioux Falls-Canton-Chicago

(See Tables 6, 8, 9)

	Daily
Lv Sioux Falls..........(No. 132)..	8.40 AM
Lv Canton...................	9.10 AM
Ar Sioux City...............	10.50 AM
Ar Manilla..................	12.50 PM
Ar Des Moines.........(Bus)..	3.25 PM
Ar Marion (Cedar Rapids) (No. 102)..	4.23 PM
Ar Savanna.................	5.47 PM
Ar Dubuque............(Bus)..	6.20 PM
Ar Chicago.........(No. 102)..	8.25 PM

Beaver Tail Drawing Room Parlor Car
Sioux Falls to Chicago [P-1020]

Tip Top Tap-Diner
Sioux City to
Chicago
Table d'hote
luncheon
and dinner
Also a la carte service. Buffet Service

Reclining Seat Lounge Coaches
Sioux Falls to Chicago

No. 4—THE PIONEER LIMITED

(See Table 1)

Milwaukee Road Station	Daily
Lv Minneapolis.................	11.10 PM
Lv St. Paul..................	11.59 PM
Lv Winona...................	1.41 AM
Lv La Crosse................	2.25 AM
Lv Portage..................	4.15 AM
Ar Milwaukee...............	6.00 AM
Lv Milwaukee...............	6.10 AM
Ar Chicago.................	8.00 AM

Parlor Car Service
Milwaukee to Chicago
Obtain Space from Pullman Conductor.

Tip Top Tap Diner
Minneapolis-St. Paul to Chicago
Buffet Service and Beverages
A la carte or club breakfast

Pullman Standard Sleeping Cars
☐ Minneapolis to Chicago
8 Duplex Roomette, 6 Roomette, 4
Double Bedrooms [44-45]
16 Duplex Roomettes-4 Double Bedrooms [41-42]

△ Minneapolis to Milwaukee
8 Duplex Roomette, 6 Roomette, 4
Double Bedrooms [47]

☐ St. Paul to Chicago
8 Duplex Roomette, 6 Roomette, 4
Double Bedrooms [46]

Reclining Seat Lounge Coaches

No. 6—THE MORNING HIAWATHA

(See Table 1)

Milwaukee Road Station	Daily
Lv Minneapolis...............	7.50 AM
Lv St. Paul.................	8.25 AM
Lv Red Wing................	9.03 AM
Lv Winona..................	9.59 AM
Lv La Crosse...............	10.33 AM
Ar Portage.................	11.54 AM
Ar Columbus................	12.20 PM
Ar Milwaukee...............	1.20 PM
Ar Chicago.................	2.40 PM

Skytop Lounge
Drawing Room Parlor Car
Minneapolis-St. Paul to Chicago [P-60]
Drawing Room Parlor Car
Minneapolis-St. Paul to Chicago [P-62]
Dining Car
Club breakfast; table d' hote luncheon
Also a la carte service
Tip Top Tap Car—Radio
Minneapolis-St. Paul to Chicago
Buffet Service and Beverages
Reclining Seat Lounge Coaches

No. 6—Aberdeen-Minneapolis

(See Table 3)

Lv Aberdeen........Daily..	9.15 PM
Lv Ortonville.......... " ..	12.23 AM
Lv Montevideo......... " ..	1.55 AM
Ar Minneapolis........ " ..	7.15 AM

Coaches
Aberdeen to Minneapolis

No. 10-2-7-56—THE COPPER COUNTRY LIMITED

(See Table 24)

	Daily
Lv Calumet. (D.S.S.& A. No.10)....	5.15 PM
Lv Houghton................	6.00 PM
Lv Champion. (Milw. Road No. 2)..	8.05 PM
Ar Channing................	9.03 PM
Lv Iron River..........(Bus)..	6.50 PM
Lv Crystal Falls...........	7.23 PM
Lv Channing.........(No. 2)..	9.15 PM
Lv Iron Mountain...........	10.00 PM
Ar Pembine................	10.20 PM
Lv Sault Ste. Marie (Soo Line No. 7)..	3.50 PM
Lv Manistique..............	7.10 PM
Lv Gladstone (Escanaba).....	8.35 PM
Ar Pembine................	10.10 PM
Lv Pembine...........(No. 2)..	10.50 PM
Lv Wausaukee..............	11.20 PM
Lv Crivitz.................	11.37 PM
Lv Green Bay...............	1.25 AM
Ar Milwaukee...............	4.10 AM
Ar Chicago..........(No. 56)..	6.20 AM

Pullman Standard Sleeping Car
⊙ Calumet to Chicago
10 Sections-Comp't-Drawing Room
[20]

Standard Sleeping Cars
⊙ Sault Ste. Marie to Chicago
10 Sections-2 Comp'ts. [22]

Dining Car Service
Sault Ste. Marie to Pembine

Reclining Seat Lounge Coaches
Calumet-Pembine to Milwaukee
Channing to Milwaukee
Milwaukee to Chicago

Coaches
Sault Ste. Marie to Pembine

No. 14—ON WISCONSIN

(See Table 18)

Milwaukee Road Station	Daily
Lv Madison.................	5.00 PM
Lv Franklin St.............	5.05 PM
Lv Watertown..............	5.55 PM
Ar Milwaukee...............	6.50 PM
Ar Chicago.................	9.40 PM

Cafe Parlor Car
Milwaukee to Chicago [P-142]
Drawing Room Parlor Car
Milwaukee to Chicago [P-140] (Sun.
Only)
Reclining Seat Lounge Coaches
Madison to Milwaukee
Milwaukee to Chicago

No. 14—THE CHIPPEWA-HIAWATHA

(See Tables 24 and 143)

Milwaukee Road Station	Daily
Lv Ontonagon..............	10 25 AM
Lv Iron Mountain...(No. 14)..	2 25 PM
Lv Menominee........(Bus)..	2.30 PM
Lv Marinette...............	2.55 PM
Lv Coleman..........(No. 14)..	3 45 PM
Lv Green Bay..............	5 05 PM
Ar Milwaukee...............	7 50 PM
Ar Chicago.................	9 40 PM

Cafe Parlor Car—Radio
Channing to Chicago [P-142]
Parlor Car
Milwaukee to Chicago [P-140] (Sun.
Only)
Dining-Buffet Service
Channing to Chicago
Buffet luncheon and table d'hote dinner.
Also a la carte service.
Reclining Seat Lounge Coaches
Ontonagon-Channing to Chicago

No. 16—THE OLYMPIAN HIAWATHA

(See Tables 1 to 5)

Milwaukee Road Station	Example	Daily
Lv Tacoma (Pacific Time)....Sun.		1.30 PM
Lv Seattle............... "		2 45 PM
Lv Spokane.............. "		10.15 PM
Lv Avery (Mountain Time)..Mon.		2.25 AM
Lv Missoula.............. "		5.50 AM
Lv Deer Lodge.......... "		7.35 AM
Lv Butte................ "		8.38 AM
Ar Three Forks.......... "		10.28 AM
Lv Three Forks.......... "		10.30 AM
Ar Harlowton............ "		1.25 PM
Lv Miles City........... "		4.50 PM
Ar Mobridge............ "		10.35 PM
Lv Mobridge (Central Time).. "		11.40 PM
Ar Aberdeen............Tue.		1.15 AM
Ar Minneapolis.......... "		6.20 AM
Lv Minneapolis.......... "		6.25 AM
Lv St. Paul............. "		7.10 AM
Ar La Crosse............ "		9.23 AM
Ar Milwaukee............ "		12.20 PM
Ar Chicago.............. "		1.45 PM

Pullman Skytop Lounge-
Sleeping Car
Tacoma-Seattle to Chicago
8 Double Bedrooms [162]
Pullman Bedroom Car
Tacoma-Seattle to Chicago
10 Roomettes-6 Double Bedrooms [161]
Touralux Sleeping Cars
Tacoma-Seattle to Chicago
14 Sections [A-16 B-16]
Dining Car
Tacoma-Seattle to Chicago
Table d'hote luncheon and dinner.
Club breakfast. Also a la carte service.
Tip-Top Grill Car
Tacoma-Seattle to Chicago
Buffet Service and Beverages
Reclining Seat Lounge Coaches
Tacoma-Seattle to Chicago
Reserved Seats

TICKETS—*The following classes of transportation will not be honored: Clergy, Charity, Employee, D.V.S., V.A.H., Blind and Attendant, Circus, Banana Messenger, Drover's, Caretaker tickets and Livestock Contracts.*

No. 18—THE COLUMBIAN

(See Tables 1 to 5)

Milwaukee Road Station	Example	Daily
Lv Tacoma.....(Pacific Time) "		8.45 PM
Lv Seattle.............. "		10.30 PM
Lv Ellensburg...........Mon.		1 55 AM
Lv Spokane.............. "		8.00 AM
Lv St. Maries........... "		9.48 AM
Ar Avery................ "		11.15 AM
Lv Avery.....(Mountain Time) "		12.25 PM
Lv Missoula............. "		4.01 PM
Lv Deer Lodge.......... "		6.00 PM
Lv Butte................ "		7.23 PM
Ar Three Forks.......... "		9.15 PM
Lv Three Forks.......... "		9.20 PM
Lv Harlowton...........Tues.		12.50 AM
Ar Mobridge............ "		12.35 PM
Lv Mobridge.....(Central Time) "		1.50 PM
Ar Aberdeen............ "		4.10 PM
Ar Minneapolis.......... "		10.35 PM
Lv Minneapolis.......... "		10.50 PM
Ar St. Paul............. "		11.37 PM
Lv St. Paul............Wed.		12.01 AM
Ar La Crosse............ "		2.45 AM
Ar Milwaukee............ "		6.55 AM
Ar Chicago.............. "		8.45 AM

Pullman Standard Sleeping Cars
Tacoma-Seattle to Chicago
6 Sections, 6 Double Bedrooms [181]
Tacoma-Seattle to Spokane
10 Sections-Buffet-Lounge [189]

Tourist Sleeping Cars
Tacoma-Seattle to Chicago
14 Sections [K-18]

Diner-Lounge Car
Tacoma-Seattle to Chicago
Club breakfast. Table d'hote luncheon
and dinner. Also a la carte service

Reclining Seat Lounge Coaches
Tacoma-Seattle to Chicago

No. 22—THE SIOUX

(See Tables 12 and 13)

Milwaukee Road Station	Daily
Lv Sioux Falls........(No. 218)..	4.00 PM
Lv Canton.................	5.30 PM
Lv Sheldon................	6.34 PM
Lv Spencer................	7.50 PM
Lv Algona.................	9.02 PM
Lv Mason City.............	10.55 PM
Lv Charles City...........	11 50 PM
Lv Calmar.................	1.40 AM
Lv Marquette..............	3.40 AM
Lv Madison................	7.00 AM
Lv Janesville.............	8.02 AM
Ar Chicago................	10.00 AM

Standard Sleeping Cars
Canton to Chicago
10 Sec.-Comp't-Drawing Room [221]
Parlor Car
Madison to Chicago [P-222]
Dining Car Service
Madison to Chicago
A la carte or club breakfast
Reclining Seat Lounge Coaches
Sioux Falls to Canton
Canton to Chicago

No. 26-108—THE SOUTHWEST LIMITED

(See Tables 10 and 11)

Union Station	Daily
Lv Kansas City.......(No. 26)..	7.30 PM
Lv Excelsior Springs......	8.07 PM
Lv Ottumwa (Sherman St.)......	12 14 AM
Ar Davenport.............	3.05 AM
Ar Savanna...............	4.45 AM
Lv Sioux Falls.......(No. 218)..	4.00 PM
Lv Sioux City......... " ..	6.45 PM
Lv Omaha............(No. 108)..	7.40 PM
Lv Des Moines.......(No. 209)..	10.20 PM
Ar Savanna...............	4.45 AM
Lv Savanna...........(No. 35)..	7.00 AM
Ar Dubuque...............	8.34 AM
Ar Freeport..........(No. 26)..	6.10 AM
Ar Beloit.................	7.08 AM
Ar Delavan...............	8.04 AM
Ar Milwaukee.............	9.45 AM
Lv Savanna..........(No. 108)..	5.20 AM
Ar Davis Jct.............	6.47 AM
Ar Chicago...............	8.50 AM

Pullman Standard Sleeping Cars
Kansas City to Chicago
10 Sec.-Comp't-Drawing Room [260]

Dining Car Service
Savanna to Chicago
A la carte or club breakfast

Reclining Seat Lounge Coaches
Kansas City-Savanna to Milwaukee
O'naha-Madrid to Savanna-Chicago
Sioux Falls-Sioux City to Savanna-
Chicago
Des Moines to Madrid
Savanna to Dubuque

⊙May be occupied until 7.00 a.m.   ☐Ready for occupancy at 9.30 p.m.   △Ready for occupancy 9.30 p.m., may be occupied until 8.00 a.m.   † Flag stop.

EQUIPMENT—EAST AND SOUTHBOUND

No. 28-12—Madison-Milwaukee-Chicago　　　(See Table 16)

Milwaukee Road Station		
Lv Madison........(No. 28) Ex. Sun....	7.50AM	
Lv Franklin St....................	7.55AM	
Lv Watertown....................	8.38AM	
Ar Milwaukee....................	9.30AM	
Lv Milwaukee......(No. 12) Daily...	9.45AM	
Ar Chicago....................	11.05AM	

Drawing Room Parlor Car
Madison to Chicago (P-285) *Ex. Sun.*

Reclining Seat Lounge Coaches
Madison to Chicago

No. 56—THE FAST MAIL　　　(See Table 1)

Milwaukee Road Station	Daily
Lv Minneapolis....................	8.20PM
Lv St. Paul....................	9.00PM
Lv Hastings....................	9.20PM
Lv Red Wing....................	9.53PM
Lv Wabasha....................	10.30PM
Lv Winona....................	11.14PM
Lv La Crosse....................	12.02AM
Lv New Lisbon....................	1.28AM
Ar Milwaukee....................	4.22AM
Ar Chicago....................	6.20AM

Pullman Standard Sleeping Car
⊙Minneapolis–St. Paul to Chicago
10 Sections–1 Drawing Room–1 Comp't. [560]

Reclining Seat Lounge Coaches
Minneapolis–St. Paul to Chicago

No. 58-14—Minneapolis-St. Paul-New Lisbon-Milwaukee-Chicago

(See Table 1)

Milwaukee Road Station	Daily
Lv Minneapolis.........(No. 58)..	9.35AM
Lv St. Paul....................	10.25AM
Lv Red Wing....................	11.18AM
Lv Winona....................	12.50PM
Lv La Crosse....................	1.53PM
Ar New Lisbon....................	3.25PM
Lv Wisconsin Dells....................	4.46PM
Lv Portage....................	5.15PM
Ar Milwaukee....................	7.40PM
Lv Milwaukee.........(No. 14)..	8.10PM
Ar Chicago....................	9.40PM

Cafe Parlor Car
Milwaukee to Chicago [142]
Drawing Room-Parlor Car
Milwaukee to Chicago [P-140] (*Sun. Only*)
Dining Car Service
Milwaukee to Chicago
Reclining Seat Lounge Coaches
Minneapolis–St. Paul to Milwaukee
Milwaukee to Chicago

No. 100—THE AFTERNOON HIAWATHA　　　(See Table 1)

Milwaukee Road Station	Daily
Lv Minneapolis....................	12.30PM
Lv St. Paul....................	1.00PM
Lv Winona....................	2.34PM
Lv La Crosse....................	3.08PM
Lv New Lisbon....................	3.57PM
Ar Portage....................	4.30PM
Ar Madison....................	6.00PM
Lv Watertown....................	5.10PM
Ar Milwaukee....................	5.55PM
Ar Chicago....................	7.15PM

Reclining Seat Lounge Coaches

Note: *Does not carry checked baggage or dogs.*

Skytop Lounge Drawing Room Parlor Car
Minneapolis–St. Paul to Chicago [P-1000]
Drawing Room-Parlor Car
Minneapolis–St. Paul to Chicago [P-1001]
Dining Car
Minneapolis–St. Paul to Chicago
Table d'hote luncheon and dinner
Al o a la carte service
Tip Top Tap Car—Radio
Minneapolis–St. Paul to Chicago
Buffet Service and Beverages

No. 102—THE MIDWEST HIAWATHA　　　(See Tables 6, 8 and 9)

Union Station	Daily
Lv Omaha.........(No. 102)..	11.55AM
Lv Council Bluffs....................	12.09PM
Lv Sioux Falls.........(No. 132)..	8.40 M
Lv Canton....................	9.10AM
Lv Sioux City....................	10.55AM
Ar Manilla....................	12.50PM
Lv Manilla.........(No. 102)..	1.14PM
Ar Madrid....................	2.31PM
Ar Des Moines.........(Bus)..	3.25PM
Lv Des Moines.........(Bus)..	1.20PM
Ar Marion (Cedar Rapids).(Bus)	4.23PM
Ar Dubuque.........(Bus)..	6.20PM
Lv Dubuque.........(Bus)..	3.45PM
Ar Savanna.........(No. 102)..	5.47PM
Ar Davis Jct....................	6.59 M
Ar Rockford.........(Bus)..	8.28 M
Ar Chicago.........(No. 102)..	8.25PM

BeaverTail Drawing Room Parlor Car
Sioux Falls–Sioux City–Manilla to Chicago [P-1020]
Tip Top Tap-Dining Car
Sioux City to Chicago
Table d'hote luncheon and dinner.
Also a la carte service. Buffet Service.
Reclining Seat Lounge Coaches
Omaha–Council Bluffs to Chicago
Sioux Falls–Sioux City to Chicago
Bus *between*
Des Moines and Madrid
Dubuque and Delmar

Note: *Does not carry checked baggage or dogs for or from Cedar Rapids.*

No. 106-6—Madison-Milwaukee-Chicago　　　(See Table 16)

Milwaukee Road Station	Daily
Lv Madison....................	11.25AM
Lv Franklin St....................	11.31AM
Lv Watertown....................	12.15PM
Ar Milwaukee....................	1.05PM
Lv Milwaukee.........(No. 6)..	1.25PM
Ar Chicago....................	2.40PM

Drawing Room Parlor Car
Madison to Milwaukee (1060) *Sun. Only*
Parlor Car
Milwaukee to Chicago
Tip Top Tap Car—Radio
Milwaukee to Chicago
Buffet Service and Beverages
Reclining Seat Lounge Coaches
Madison to Milwaukee
Milwaukee to Chicago

No. 108—THE ARROW　　　(See Tables 6, 8 and 9)

Union Station	Daily
Lv Omaha.........(No. 108)..	7.40PM
Lv Council Bluffs....................	7.55PM
Ar Manilla....................	9.20PM
Lv Sioux Falls.........(No. 218)..	4.00PM
Lv Sioux City....................	6.45PM
Ar Manilla....................	9.20PM
Lv Manilla.........(No. 108)..	9.50PM
Ar Madrid....................	11.42PM
Ar Des Moines.........(No. 208)..	4.05AM
Lv Des Moines.........(No. 209)..	10.20PM
Lv Madrid.........(No. 108)..	12.01AM
Lv Marion....................	2.41AM
Ar Savanna....................	4.55AM
Lv Savanna.........(No. 35)..	7.00AM
Ar Dubuque....................	8.34AM
Ar Freeport.........(No. 26)..	6.10AM
Ar Beloit....................	7.08AM
Ar Milwaukee....................	9.45AM
Lv Savanna.........(No. 108)..	5.20AM
Ar Davis Jct....................	6.47AM
Ar Chicago....................	8.50AM

Pullman Bedroom Lounge Car
Sioux Falls–Sioux City to Chicago
6 Single–2 Double Bedrooms [1080]
Pullman Standard Sleeping Cars
Omaha–Council Bluffs to Chicago
8 Sections–2 Comp'ts–Drawing Room [1081]
Sioux Falls–Sioux City to Chicago
12 Sec.–Drawing Room [1082]
Dining Buffet Service
Sioux Falls–Sioux City to Manilla
Table d'hote or a la carte dinner
Savanna to Chicago
Reclining Seat Lounge Coaches
Omaha–Madrid to Chicago
Sioux Falls–Sioux City to Chicago
Savanna to Milwaukee
Savanna to Dubuque
Des Moines to Madrid

No. 118—THE VARSITY　　　(See Table 16)

Milwaukee Road Station	Daily
Lv Madison....................	5.05PM
Lv Janesville....................	6.01PM
Ar Chicago....................	7.50PM

Cafe Parlor Car
Madison to Chicago [P-1180]
Table d'hote dinner
Also a la carte service
Buffet Service and Beverages
Reclining Seat Lounge Coaches
Madison to Chicago

No. 122-22—THE SIOUX　　　(See Tables 7 and 12)

Milwaukee Road Station	Daily
Lv Austin.........(No. 122)..	10.30PM
Lv Calmar.........(No. 22)..	1.40AM
Lv Madison....................	7.00AM
Lv Janesville....................	8.02AM
Ar Chicago....................	10.00AM

Pullman Sleeping Car
□ Austin to Chicago (*Ex. Sat.*)
8 Sections–2 Comp'ts–Drawing Room [1220]
Parlor Car
Madison to Chicago [P-222]
Dining Car Service
Madison to Chicago
A la carte or club breakfast
Reclining Seat Lounge Coaches
Austin to Calmar
Calmar to Chicago

No. 200-100—THE HIAWATHA—North Woods Service　　　(See Table 23)

	Daily
Lv Woodruff....................	10.40AM
Lv Minocqua....................	10.50AM
Lv Wausau.........(No. 200)..	1.01PM
Lv Mosinee....................	1.25PM
Lv Junction City....................	1.48PM
Lv Wisconsin Rapids....................	2.15PM
Ar New Lisbon....................	3.35PM
Lv New Lisbon (No. 100)....................	3.57PM
Ar Portage....................	4.30PM
Ar Madison.........(No. 700)..	6.00PM
Lv Portage....................	4.32PM
Ar Milwaukee....................	5.55PM
Ar Chicago....................	7.15PM

Cafe Parlor Car
Woodruff–Minocqua to New Lisbon [P-2000]
Drawing Room Parlor Cars
New Lisbon to Chicago [P-1000–P-1001]
Dining and Buffet Service
Woodruff–Minocqua to New Lisbon
New Lisbon to Chicago
Table d'hote luncheon and dinner
Al o a la carte service.
Reclining Seat Lounge Coaches
Woodruff–Minocqua to New Lisbon
New Lisbon to Portage–Chicago
Portage to Madison

Note: *Does not carry checked baggage or dogs, New Lisbon to Madison–Chicago, and between Minocqua and New Lisbon Sunday only.*

No. 218-108-208—Sioux Falls-Sioux City-Madrid-Des Moines　　　(See Tables 6 and 9)

Milwaukee Road Station	
Lv Sioux Falls.........(No. 218)..	4.00PM
Lv Sioux City....................	6.45PM
Ar Manilla....................	9.20PM
Ar Manning.........(No. 108)..	10.09PM
Ar Madrid....................	11.42PM
Lv Madrid.........(No. 208)..	3.05AM
Ar Des Moines....................	4.05AM

Dining Buffet Service
Sioux Falls–Sioux City to Manilla
Table d'hote or a la carte dinner
Reclining Seat Lounge Coaches
Sioux Falls–Sioux City to Madrid
Madrid to Des Moines

No. 256-56 and No. 202-56—THE TOMAHAWK　　　(See Table 23)

Milwaukee Road Station	Daily Ex. Sun.	Sun. only
Lv Minocqua..(No. 256)..	6.30PM	7.20PM
Lv Tomahawk....................	7.29PM	8.21PM
Lv Wausau....................	9.15PM	9.30PM
Lv Mosinee....................	9.42PM	9.55PM
Lv Wisconsin Rapids....................	10.40PM	10.48PM
Lv New Lisbon (No. 56)..	1.28AM	1.28AM
Lv Portage....................	2.24AM	2.24AM
Ar Milwaukee....................	4.35AM	4.35AM
Ar Chicago....................	6.20AM	6.20AM

Standard Sleeping Cars
⊙Minocqua to Chicago
10 Sections–Comp't–Drawing Room [2560]
△Minocqua to Milwaukee
10 Sections–Comp't–Drawing Room [2561] *Ex. Sat.*
Reclining Seat Lounge Coaches
Minocqua to Chicago

f Stops on signal to take or leave passengers.　**⊙** May be occupied until 7.00 a.m.　**△** May be occupied until 8.00 a.m.　**□** Ready for occupancy at 9.30 p.m.

INDEX

174